Fishing for Lake Lanier
Striped Bass

ISBN: 1-4563-4824-8
ISBN-13: 978-1456348243

Fishing for Lake Lanier Striped Bass

Capt Tom Blackburn
With Contributions From
Capt Chuck Kizina

2011

CONTENTS

Foreword

The savage strike, the ensuing surge, and the tremendous display of pound for pound strength provide the ultimate Lanier fishing experience. Just the sight of your rod tip buried in the water is a thrill.

Once you have experienced this rush you will return an endless number of times to experience what is undeniably one of the most addictive sports in the world. Without doubt, this helps to explain the exponential growth in the number of Striper aficionados on Lake Lanier

The Striper fishery on Lake Sidney Lanier is healthy and a year-round source of fun. Unlike our northern fishing friends, we are not frozen over for part of the year! If you are properly prepared, the fishing action is non-stop. In the pages that follow, we hope to help you by offering some of our understanding of the striped bass, our thoughts on evaluating and optimizing your boat and gear, understanding bait and fishing techniques and putting it all together. There are no secrets here, just making the best of what you have and getting out there to put it into practice.

Thank you for taking some of your time to read this book and we hope you will enjoy it and find it useful. Everything you read is based on our experiences as avid striper fishermen. We fully expect that you will agree with some of it and hopefully find some useful information and techniques that will help you catch a few more fish. We expect that you will disagree with some of it as well.

Hey, that's fishing for you.

We hope that you enjoy this book as much as we enjoyed writing it.

I
Introduction

Fishing for striped bass in Lake Sidney Lanier is an addictive pastime. This book was written to be your companion and guide to preparing yourself and your equipment for some of the most exciting fishing in the southeastern United States.

The Striper fishery in Lake Lanier is robust, resulting from years of stocking and the availability of high quality food for the fish in the form of shad, herring and various other pan-fish. The lake is easily accessible and a pleasure to fish, especially in the off season, when many of the recreational boaters are off the lake waiting for that well known Hotlanta weather.

Every fisherman can find some gems of information in these pages from basic techniques to advanced ones. Not every fisherman spends every day on the water or has a boat set up for striper fishing only. There are even some techniques that are seen as cutting edge on Lake Lanier that have been used by fishermen on the great lakes for years. This book is part of that evolution too.

To be successful, you have to make the best of what you have and come up with a plan. Your plan may be what you are going to do tomorrow, deciding on a new type of hook, or where you need to put another rod holder. It may even include buying a new boat. Everybody is different.

So keep in mind that there are many ways to catch a trophy fish, because a trophy fish means something different to everyone that fishes. It can be the trophy gained from working years to catch a fish breaking the lake record or experiencing the rewarding moment of helping someone catch their first striper on a day spent with friends on the lake.

Luck is where preparedness meets opportunity. Use this book to plan and prepare for what may be some of the most memorable fishing days in your entire life.

II
Making the Most of your Boat and Gear

The best thing about striper fishing is that there are many ways to catch a fish. You can fish from the shore or a boat, in the spring, summer, winter or fall, with live bait or artificial, with your friends or by yourself. To become a successful fisherman, meaning becoming someone that can catch a few fish when nobody else is catching any, you will have to work at it. I would bet that you think about and plan your fishing for as many or more hours than you actually have a line in the water. If you don't now, eventually you will.

Every journey has a beginning, middle and end. For this journey we begin by embarking together on a path that will hopefully help your fishing success and pleasure. For the first steps, it makes good sense to figure out what you will be able to do best. The best way to do that is to start with what you have.

Your boat & gear—maximizing what you have

For the time being, let's assume that you have a boat and some fishing gear, or, that maybe one of your friends has a boat and gear and you can influence how it is set up. Anyway, most striper fishing on Lake Lanier is from a boat and this book focuses on boat based techniques.

It is important to keep in mind that nobody has a boat that is perfect for everything. Actually, probably every boat has something that has to be adjusted every day to get the most out of your fishing efforts. That is a lot of the fun.

The same goes for your rods, reels and the contents of your tackle box. No single rig will work everywhere, every time. With that said, if you keep your gear in good maintenance and keep your hooks sharp, you will do fine. A new shiny reel does not make you a great fisherman, a great fisherman is made by paying attention to the details, study and practice.

Always strive to maximize what you have and fish to your strengths, if you do this, you will be far more successful. A good place to start is to think about your boat, or the boat you are dreaming about. So let's get into some detail by proposing some ideas and thoughts about the major things that you will need to consider.

A Lake Lanier Striper Boat

A dandy Lake Lanier Striper boat should be able to be rigged in some way for down-lining, planer boards, flat-lining, and trolling. This will enable you to take advantage of the year-round fishing that Lake Lanier offers. During certain months of the year you will be down-lining *and* pulling planer boards *and* flat-lines at the same time. Study the layout of your boat and begin to envision where and how you plan to fish up to four planer boards, two flat-lines, and two down-lines simultaneously. You won't be doing this often, but there are times you will want to use every method you can muster. And hey, if you don't tangle a few lines, you ain't fishin'!

It is not important that you have a specific type of boat. There are ways to rig a center console, pontoon, skiff, hardtop salmon boat, and many other designs into an effective fishing platform. It just takes thought and planning.

Think about strategically locating your rod holders to accommodate rods rigged for these various techniques. There are a variety of rod holders on the market, so pick good sturdy ones. One piece of equipment that may facilitate this is the T-Bar from Driftmaster. Although it can hold up to four rods, you are best prepared by attaching two rod holders to each T-Bar. The T-Bar can be attached to your boat in one of two ways: by using a star base or by purchasing the model that includes the flush mount which will fit into an existing flush-mounted rod holder. In any case, be sure that your rod holders are of good quality and sturdily mounted. These holders accommodate many different sizes of rods easily and it is quite easy to remove your rod from one when a striper is pretty much trying to yank your rod out of your hands at the same time.

If you have a center console boat with a T-top, you will have an advantage over other boats in that rod holders for planer boards may be mounted on the aluminum rail frame of the T-top. Look to see if you can mount two rod holders on each side of the T-top pointing outward, tilted a little above horizontal.

Most T-tops also have rod holders for storage on the back side—these are commonly called rocket launchers. Using the rocket launchers for flat lines doesn't work too well unless you are using some form of a float, as they hold the rods upright decreasing your ability to effectively get your line in the water. Simply said, you are starting off too high from the water. A better idea is that you would use an existing rod holder or the rod holder with a T-Bar for flat-lines. You're right—not everybody owns a boat with a T-Top. So, what about those folks who do not have one? How do they rig for planer boards?

Well, if you are going to fish eight lines, you will need eight rod holders. If you are fishing two lines, then two it is. Again, some of the rod holders may be attached to a T-Bar to increase your ability to use more rods. Boats having an aluminum rail around the windshield lend themselves to rod holders spotted around the rail. In other cases, the rod holders should be mounted on rails and gunnels. In this final process of placing the rod holders on the gunnel or rail, take into consideration rod holder placement as it relates to trolling lead-core and umbrella rigs. In those cases where you must permanently install a rod holder, attempt to locate it for two purposes; first for planer boards and second for trolling artificial lures with the main engine. Yes, with the main engine.

Let me explain that. Throughout part of a fishing year, you will be trolling artificial lures or umbrella rigs using the main engine for propulsion, not your trolling motor. It is an issue of speed and controllability. You are mimicking the speed and motion of a school of darting fish as you zigzag around the lake. Generally, during these times you would troll no more than two umbrella rigs or two lead-core lines.

There is another important thing to consider. You should also think about the times you may fish by yourself. In these cases, maybe placing a rod holder that is six to eighteen inches toward the bow from your position at the helm you can fish by yourself and visibly monitor each rod. Switching from looking ahead to behind you all of the time can be tiring.

A good amount of successful fishermen fish the lake trolling with down-riggers. How do you do that? Or, more specifically, how do you attach the down rigger to your boat? That will depend on your boat's construction and layout.

The easiest way other than a permanently mount a down-rigger is to have a flush-mount rod holder installed in the gunnel and to have a corresponding flush mount base attached to the down rigger. If your boat does not have a flush mount holder, you could attach the base of the rigger directly to the gunnel with screws/bolts. There is an advantage to come up with a way to mount them so they can be removed when you are not using them or if you are storing your boat. A handy thing to keep in mind is that because most down riggers use steel wire, you will hear the wire "sing" as it passes through the water. Should this annoy you, you can revert to one of the most useful tools on earth—second of course only to duct tape—a bungee cord. Placing it around the wire and a stationary object on the boat should reduce the singing.

Before going too far, I know you are already thinking about storing all of these rods. Rod storage is an issue we face every day. On a typical December day, a well equipped striper boat might take a minimum of twelve rod/reels, pre rigged for—four planer boards, two flat-lines, four downlines, and two umbrellas. Think out the best way to store the rods safely and out of the way until you need to use them. Never leave loose rods on the deck, they will get broken, kicked into the water or worse—trip you and put you in the water too.

If you have a separate, non-attached bait tank, you can purchase or construct a rod holder consisting of plastic tubes attached together with nylon webbing which wraps around your bait tank. A second option is to purchase or construct a rod holder system around a pedestal and plastic rod holder. The primary goal is safety. For example, storing your casting rods outfitted with large treble hook laden lures in such a manner that the hooks are at chest or head height, well, you are asking for a trip to the emergency room. Remember that your guests on your boat may not be savvy about thinking about hooks when they move about your boat, especially when fishing at night or when they are excited about catching a few Stripers!

Second is being able to fish around all of the rods. It makes more sense to store your unused rods either up and out of the way, or near the center of the boat. Think about if you are playing a fish and it circles your boat. You need to follow it around without going up and over a bunch of rods stored around the edges of your boat.

I can just hear you still thinking about those twelve rods. Here are your thoughts: first, twelve rods & reels can be outside my budget and even if I had the money, there is insufficient storage space on my boat. In this situation creativity and ingenuity should prevail. First, it is fairly easy to convert a flat line to a down-line and vice versa; so, you should consider this idea. With a little luck, you may be able convert two of your rods/reels for umbrella rig trolling. Think about it for a while. Hey, you can always start with a few less rods and add more later on. Oh, and learn to tie good knots quickly.

There are some other mechanical systems on your boat that you have to think about in order to use all of that fishing equipment you are carrying around.

To effectively fish with down-lines, planer boards, and flat-lines, you need to move slowly and under con-trol. This is where a trolling motor becomes essential. You should plan on using an electric trolling motor which can be powered by 12, 24, or 36 volts. On Lake Lanier, the most widely used trolling motor for a striper boat is powered by 24 volts. Trolling motors are measured by the amount of "thrust" they provide. For a 24 ft. center console, you may require a minimum of 80 pounds while a fifteen foot bass boat may be able to use 55 pounds. A general rule of thumb is to acquire a trolling motor that provides more thrust than you think is necessary. Better to have it and not need it than need it and not have it.

As you might guess, trolling motors come in different shaft lengths. Normally, the greatest length is sixty inches. While your center console may not need a sixty inch shaft on a day-to-day basis, think about those days in which 18 knot winds picks up the water, and pitches the boat so that the entire trolling motor is lifted in and out of the water thus making your fishing ineffective.

If you go with a 60 inch shaft on a center console boat you won't be disappointed. Bass boats and other vessels having a lower bow can get by with a 54 inch shaft. One other thing, most trolling motors are equipped with a depth collar which is a movable clamp on the shaft of the motor. You can always adjust to a shorter length. The depth collar can be used in more calm waters by lowering it on the shaft and thus reducing the length of the shaft in the water.

Speaking of trolling motor shafts, it's wise to periodically inspect your trolling motor. Look for cracks in the shaft and evidence of stress in the propeller. Does the propeller spin without "wobble"? Is there any indication that water is in the shaft and possibly the motor housing? Boaters should always be cognizant of the locking device on the trolling motor. If you improperly stow the trolling motor and navigate across the lake, there is an excellent chance that the shaft/motor will fall away from the stowed position into the water. Should this occur, there is a good chance the trolling motor will require some extensive repairs, if you are lucky enough to find it!

As you invest more into a trolling motor, you get more options. Trolling motors can be equipped with software that enables it to follow a course you select. Currently on the market there is a "copilot" as well as an "autopilot". As its name implies, autopilot responds to the direction established by using the remote control. The motor will continue to use the original heading unless it receives another signal or the operator disengages the process. Copilot results in the same thing but the intended heading may need to be changed based on wind, boat captain preferences, etc.

Your electric trolling motor is your year-round workhorse. Its importance cannot be overemphasized. While there are many types of trolling motors, here are some considerations. First and in most cases, the average Striper fisherman can use a bow-mounted motor. Assuming a bow mounted motor; do you want to go with a hand control which requires your presence on the bow or the remote controlled motor? Experience points to considering a remote controlled unit. With a remote controlled unit, the Captain can control the boat's direction and speed from anywhere on the boat with a wireless controller that fits in your hand or pocket.

Assuming you have one sonar/GPS unit and its location is near the helm, you should use the wireless remote controlled unit from there. While using the remote from the helm, you can best monitor speed and direction, which are critical components of a successful day on the Lake.

Trolling motors draw power from deep cycle batteries that require periodic charging and maintenance. In some cases, your trolling motor will be hard-wired directly to the batteries.

Conversely, some fishermen prefer to use a plug that can be easily disconnected. In both cases, it is very important to maintain vigilance over the batteries. Terminals must be clean and free of rust; otherwise, they will be difficult to charge and they will not deliver sufficient voltage thus cutting short your day on the lake. The bottom line is to make sure you use batteries designed for trolling and maintain your system.

The deep cycle batteries require a charger—most of the time one that is on-board linked to a 120 volt outlet. You can opt for a two, three, or four battery charger. A four battery charger can be used to charge two trolling and two cranking batteries.

Where possible and it makes sense, stretch your budget and purchase the four battery charger. You should also consider another issue when purchasing a battery charger—evaluate the total output to each battery. At a minimum, use the ten amp per battery charger; the preferred charger will deliver 15 amps to each battery. This issue is important to striper fishermen who may fish every day. Picture this…your in-laws are in town for a week of fishing. They know you are a successful striper fisherman. So, on Monday it's you and the in-laws. After a good day of fishing, you connect your ten amp, onboard charger. Before you leave for the Lake early the next day, you check the status of your batteries by looking at the charger which indicates that the batteries are not fully charged. (Green lights on the charger typically indicate that the batteries are fully charged). You see they have not had time to fully charge. That could be trouble, especially if you run out of battery power right when you are on the fish. Want to bet you will never hear the end of it?

For those fishermen who will be on the lake on a day-to-day basis and have a choice between a fifteen or ten amp charger, purchase the fifteen amp charger.

How many cranking batteries do you need? You should consider two cranking batteries assuming of course your boat allows for sufficient space for two. Why two cranking batteries? Many fishermen literally load-up a boat with equipment: two sonar/GPS units, two bait tanks each with a power bubbler system, lights, bait tank pumps, etc. Please note that your sonar unit requires a fully charged battery. In those cases where your cranking battery is not fully charged, your sonar unit will periodically cut-off and on and it can also lose its position with respect to the satellites.

How can you protect your electrical system—specifically the cranking batteries? Install a Dual Battery Switch. The advantage of the Switch is that for periods in which you will not be using your boat, you can select the "Off" position on the switch which will prevent any electrical device on the boat from draining your batteries.

When does something small become a big issue? You're on the Lake and your cell phone battery is discharged. How are you going to communicate with all of your network members to find out where the fish are today? What about safety issues? One solution is to install at least one if not two cigarette plugs. Phone chargers draw very little amperage and should be considered a "must" for your boat and…don't forget your charge cord.

Early one morning, after launching the boat and attempting to turn on the sonar/GPS unit, I quickly determined that the unit was not going to come on. All of my efforts were unsuccessful so, I made a u-turn and put the boat back on the trailer. That's how much I rely on my electronics! No electronics—No Go!

Electronics which offer information relative to mapping, lake contours, and depth provide boaters with extremely valuable information with respect to navigation, shallow water and boating obstructions. Outside of your experience, skills, judgment, common sense and your visual acuity, the sonar/GPS unit is a great source of navigation information. Think of the unit as a fully functional tool and it is under your command.

The bottom line is to think about how to equip your boat to be versatile, effective and most of all, safe. Spend a lot of time looking at other striper boats like yours, and some not like yours. You will get plenty of ideas from that too.

Make sure you periodically evaluate when you may have too much gear on the boat. Sometimes achieving the balance between well equipped and equipment overload is a fine line. By re-evaluating your style and resources from time to time, you will achieve good balance. Most fishermen start simply, move into some level of having too much gear, then simplify to what they like and need. It is the nature of things.

Bait tank

Bait tanks can range from twenty to sixty gallons. Some are built into the boat, some are not. Some are simply a cooler.

Obviously, larger tanks are better for the bait. A filtration system would be a big plus. A filtration system can consist of two chambers—one containing charcoal and a second chamber filled with a substance that looks like it could be used to fill a pillow case. The purpose of the filtration system is to catch bait scales and to keep the water clean. Scales will considerably shorten the life of your bait.

The purpose of an aeration system is to pump air, which is 21 percent oxygen, into the bait tank. A good working aeration system is essential.

More aeration is obviously better. An aeration system consists of an air pump, tubing, and one or more diffusers (air stones). The aeration system can be powered by the twelve volt system (cranking batteries). Some extra large bait tanks may require two separate aeration systems.

Please note that the aeration pump, when connected to the cranking battery, may cause excessive and undesirable "noise" which may reduce the quality of the picture of your sonar unit. If this should occur, consider changing the source of power to the trolling batteries.

There is another form of aeration system worthy of consideration—this system consists of a converter to convert the power from twelve volts to 120 volts, a 120 volt air pump, and a large air stone. Not only can this system be used during your fishing session, it can be used to maintain bait over a period of one to three days depending on the type of bait. In that case, you could connect the air pump directly to a 120 volt outlet.

Some aeration systems and pumps move the water and create a current in your tank; please note that Blueback Herring do not necessarily enjoy moving water.

If you are using a cooler for your bait tank, think about figuring out a way to keep enough oxygen in the water. An air stone can help you accomplish this or if you have the money, a portable oxygen tank with a micro-pore stone is even better.

If you are installing or using a portable bait tank, make sure you position your bait tank in a location that is accessible, and fixed so it does not unbalance your boat. Lively bait is very important to successful fishing. There will be more on managing and using your tank later.

Rods & Reels

There are many theories and opinions out there as to what rod & reel combination makes the best striper rod. The good thing is that you don't need an expensive rod & reel to be successful. For the most part, your down-lining rods will be spooled up with 20 pound main line with a variety of leaders, depending on the season and technique you are employing at the time. This means you will be selecting a medium weight rod. As far as length, somewhere around 8 feet will work fine. Look for a rod that is flexible and not too stiff. The sensitivity that a graphite rod offers will not be optimal for striper fishing from a boat so look for something tougher. Fiberglass rods are fine. If you fish with friends that are prone to reeling your weight or swivel into the rod tip, think about metal guides or rig a design that will take the abuse by putting a bead on the line above your swivel.

Another type of rod & reel you will use will be slightly heavier and a bit shorter for your lead-core and umbrella rig fishing. If you stay with you lighter rods for this type of fishing, you will not be as happy as your rod will be bent over from the weight of your line or rig before you even hook a fish. The reel will be a bit larger too so you can accommodate the heavier equipment and line. Whether you purchase a reel with a counter or not is up to you. They are handy, but you can do without one as well.

Graphite rods are nice but you have to be careful not to use rods that are too stiff or brittle. They are for a different purpose, where you have to feel a light bite. If you are trolling with your prized custom graphite rod and it gets snagged at precisely the moment you can't get to it in time, you run the risk of breaking it in half. Not a good scenario under any circumstances. Pricey too.

For the times when fish are surfacing near you, you should always have a lighter weight casting rod set up with something to throw. One of the most exciting moments fishing will be when you are trolling slowly and a school of striper surfaces all around you. It happens every so often. You are in the right place at the right time. This is the moment when you have to grab that surface lure and get it out there! You need a setup for that. You will kick yourself if you don't. That is experience talking.

Don't forget that you can throw that lure behind a fish that someone else is reeling in. Often it will be a larger fish jumping into the fracas to see if they can get some of the scraps that they think will be falling off as the first fish is feeding. They don't know that the other fish is being reeled in by you and they have gotten quite lazy and big over the years by letting the younger fish do most of the work preparing their food.

It pays to mention that your reels should be in good operating condition. Learn to service them yourself or know a friend that will do it for you. If you buy quality reels, and service them, they will last you a lifetime. A few tools, grease, oil and time will be all that you will need. Nothing fancy. Grease gears, oil on the rest. Do it while watching one of your favorite fishing shows.

Pay particular attention to reels known for a smooth drag and can take the abuse of long runs. Lake Lanier stripers can reach over 40 inches and they can work over a reel overheating it pretty quickly. If your reel heats up and your drag gets sticky or jumpy, you can break your line. It is an easily avoided problem. Get good stuff and take care of it. Losing a prize fish because of an unmaintained reel is your fault—and your fault alone.

Hooks

An entire book can be written about the selection of hooks. Regardless of your selected type, keeping a variety of sizes of that particular hook so if your bait size changes, you can use the appropriate size hook.

Probably the most popular trolling hooks are the ones designed for keeping the bait centered on the hook so the bait does not have the ability to foul hook itself and pull through the water in an unnatural way. Second to these style hooks are the octopus and circle hook varieties. These hooks are well suited for striper fishing and once the fish is hooked, they stay in place.

As far as color of the hook is concerned, there are fishermen that swear that red hooks are better, there are fishermen that swear that black hooks are better and there are fishermen that swear that shiny hooks are better.

Try to figure that one out. It is more than likely that a fisherman is more prone to use their favorite hook more often. And what they use most often catches the most fish! Simple as that.

Most of all, if a hook does not have a very, very sharp point, it is useless. If it is dull, sharpen it or throw it out. If it is rusty, throw it out. In the grand scheme of things, hooks are cheap.

Fishhooks have been around for a long time. They are pretty simple. From the eye, shank, point, barb, bend, and gap, you must understand that the most important part of the hook is the point. Whether it is a needle point, rolled in point, or a hollow point, it must be razor sharp. Some anglers use the term sticky sharp, meaning if you drag the point lightly across your fingernail, it should catch a bit and dig into your fingernail some, feeling "sticky". If you test your hook this way and the point just slides on your fingernail, it is not sharp.

Hook sizes are determined by numbers. Smaller hooks are numbered from 32 to 1 with a size 32 hook being extremely small. After size 1, hook sizes increase and are numbered 1/0 to 19/0.

Most hooks are manufactured from steel and covered with a rust-resistant surface coating. Hooks may also be coated with a color such as red, gold, nickel, etc. Some are made from stainless steel.

When shopping for hooks, you will note that there are many styles. Hooks have different shapes, materials, points and barbs and eye type. While there are many colors, shapes, and types, most Lanier Striper fishermen either use a Bait-Keeper, Kahle, Circle, or Octopus hook. When live bait fishing any of these may be used; cut-bait fishing lends itself to circle or octopus hooks.

The hook that delivers the highest catch ratio with the least rate of gut hooking is the Circle hook which is sharply curved in a circular shape. How does the Circle hook work and why is it so successful? The answer lies with its design. When a Striper inhales your Blueback Herring, it uses its tongue and the force of the water to turn the bait head first as it enters the stomach. This takes place in less than one second! Anyway, as the fish turns, the hook is disengaged from the Herring and because it is curved, it slides back out of the stomach. This is where the design of the hook comes into play. The hook departs the stomach as your line pulls on it and as soon as it meets an exposed surface (the fish's jaw & lip), the point meets this surface and you have a "hook-up". Normally, the hook-up occurs in the corner of the mouth. On a true circle hook, the hook will work itself completely around the jaw bone, making it nearly impossible for the fish to become unhooked.

When using a circle hook, remember this phrase, "Crank not yank!" The combination of the circle hook, quality leader, base line and a soft-tipped rod provide the perfect setting for a solid hook-up. There is no need to "set the hook". As a matter of fact, the act of setting the hook while using a circle hook will more than likely result in the hook being pulled out of the mouth of the Striper!

Swivels

The most important thing to say about swivels is to use good quality swivels. If you buy cheap swivels or use old nasty jammed up ones, you are only asking for trouble. Swivels are important as they protect your line against twisting when you are pulling bait. Sometimes a Herring will foul hook itself and spin. This spinning action will twist your line quickly, something that must be avoided. Ball bearing swivels are really great when you get them. Also, size them appropriately to your line test. Not too big, not too small. Tie them on to the main line with a Palomar knot.

Bead

Just above your swivel, it pays in some instances to install a small bead to protect your rod tip from the action of reeling a swivel into the rod tip, damaging it. This same bead can serve the purpose of stopping your planer board from sliding down to your line, past the swivel and to your hook. It is one thing trying to bring in a striper with a planer board halfway up your line. It is quite another to be reeling in a prize fish and your planer board as it slides down the line and passes the swivel, goes down your leader and is now bouncing on the nose of one quite agitated fish. You had better hold on and hope that board does not give the added bit of leverage the fish needs to break free.

Leader

Carefully select your leader. The length will vary and the weight will vary depending on the type of fishing you are doing. Fluorocarbon leader is nice to have as it is arguably less visible in the water. However, it is a bit stiffer and some folks say more susceptible to nicks. These nicks cause weak spots which can be the cause of a line break when reeling in a fish. Hey, a nick will weaken any monofilament line so don't let that scare you off the stuff.

The important point is that you really have to make sure that your leader is in tip-top shape when you put it in the water. Every time.

III
BAIT

A little thought about live bait can't hurt. The best way to understand it is to start with a little history about live bait and Lake Lanier.

The History of Live Bait in Lake Lanier

The illegal introduction of the Blueback Herring to the lake in the 1990s had significant effects on both the Lake and its fishermen. Without Herring in the summer, fishermen were confined to lead-core and down-rigger trolling. In the cooler months, fishermen could use Threadfin and Gizzard Shad, shiners, and minnows and, of course, artificial lures. With the exception of shiners, you had to know how to use a cast net and where to throw it for shad.

You got wet and cold and there were no guarantees you could find or catch your bait. Those who were able to catch fresh bait with a cast net had to learn through years of hard gained experience of the various techniques required to maintain bait in tanks. From an historical perspective, the technology and related improvements to onboard bait tanks has been significant.

What a surprise it must have been for a cast net thrower in 1999-2000 when he saw a couple of blueback Herring in his net! I can hear him now, "What the........." I know it was a big surprise for me when catching them in a net in the back of Flat Creek. As they were flopping on the front deck of my boat, my buddy and I were trying to identify what they were. Sometimes you caught four or more dozen in one throw! It did not take long before we realized that they were the smaller-sized version of the Herring we used to net on the Chesapeake.

Most of the issues related to the blueback Herring were addressed when the State Department of Natural Resources ruled it was legal to use the Herring on Lanier. Oh boy, changes were upon us!

Bait shops wanted to carry them but had to learn more about keeping them lively. Fishermen wanted to learn more about the Herring and how to keep them alive on their boat in heat of the summer. Initially, most of us had problems in the early 2000s keeping the bait in good shape. We struggled to learn more about the proper maintenance of the Herring. We learned through our mistakes. As fall approached in the first year the use of Herring was legal, the retail price of Herring in some establishments was $12 per dozen and as I wrote above, keeping the Herring alive during the day was "iffy"; accordingly, many Lanier fishermen took-up the art of cast-net throwing. It seemed that everyone became a cast net specialist during this period. It was very much a time of learning and experimentation.

When the use of Herring became legal, the increase in the number of Striper fishermen on Lanier was exponential. Striper fishing clubs were formed and forums were started. Fishermen started to communicate with each other and over time learned some of the techniques required to maintain the Herring. Sales of center console boats increased on the lake and at one time there were twenty one dealers in this boat market! The retail sales price for Herring decreased and this also was a factor in the increase of Lanier striper fishermen.

But after all of the above events occurred, many of us struggled with the Herring. In the beginning, we did not know what the water temperature should be in our bait tank. When the water seemed to be too warm, we sometimes dumped an excessive amount of ice in the water which quickly and quite effectively stunned them. We also noticed excessive loss of scales and did not initially understand the significance of this. Adding to that, the ice we were using contained chlorine which shortened the life of the bait. The water from some of the bait shops contained chlorine and other trace chemicals and we did not know the proper remedial treatment of the water. I think you're getting the point.

So, after all these years, one would think that all Striper fishermen would know all of the "dos and don'ts" and would be very successful in the maintenance of his blue-back Herring.

Unfortunately, this is not the case; as a matter of fact, some folks are still struggling with this issue.

As recent as the summer of 2009, I received numerous phone calls from the owner of the retail establishment selling Herring. Here is the typical mid-morning cell-phone conversation, "Hey, how's your bait doing?" Response: "Just fine—we have boated several Stripers and the bait is very active". Bait salesman, "The guy behind you in line this morning purchased four dozen and he just called me to say that all of the Herring are dead!"

At this point, there is silence on my end because I cannot understand why the Herring perished so quickly.

As an analytical person, there is a great desire to investigate, ask questions, inspect the bait tank, etc. From experience, we have learned that as new Striper fishermen enter the market, they experience the same frustration the "Old Timers" did in the early 90s.

Some of these new folks on the Lake are not asking questions, joining forums, or joining Striper fishing clubs. As a result, they don't have much help becoming knowledgeable of the basic bait-maintenance techniques. This leads them to frustration, dissatisfaction, and, in some cases, defeat! Learning is key. Hey, recommend this book to them! It can't hurt.

The goal in these next sections is to tackle all facets of bait including bait acquisition, bait maintenance, bait use, bait tanks, new technology affecting bait, and how to make sure that your bait will be inviting to that trophy Striper you seek!

Purchasing Bait

When purchasing bait from a retail establishment, it behooves you to ask several questions. First, what is the source of the water—does it have Chlorine in it? If you are using water from the retailer, learn what the water temperature is. When bringing bait from the holding tank, ask the attendant to place no more than two dozen in a five-gallon bucket. Do not overcrowd the Herring in the buckets. If possible, fill your bait tank completely to avoid bait "sloshing".

Examine the bait in your tank before you leave the store and remove the Herring that are swimming upside down, those having black backs and those with a red nose. Keep the lid closed on the bait tank during the trip to the ramp or from the establishment to your dock. Do your best to make their ride as stress free as possible.

Catching bait with a Net

Notwithstanding the availability of bait at the retail level, there are some fishermen who have committed themselves to the practice of catching bait with their net; some of the new folks on Lanier are following their lead.

Going forward with the purchase of a net, you should first consider the bait you intend to catch. For instance, to catch Threadfin Shad and Blueback Herring, purchase a mono net with a one quarter inch mesh having 1.25 to 1.5 pounds of lead weight per radius foot. Almost every winter, there will be a period of time in which the Stripers will focus on small Threadfin Shad. Because it is rare for bait shops to sell threadfins, you may consider purchasing a net to catch them. Assuming you have room, store a bucket and the net on your boat.

As to catching Herring and Threadfins, both species are attracted to light. If you can find a dock on the lake with a sodium or similar light that is illuminated during the night, take a close look at the water around the light. In most cases, some bait will be under the light. During the day, catching Threadfins and Herring becomes more difficult. At night and just before dawn, you will find Herring near the bank. On a calm day in winter, you can see threadfins on the surface; more than likely you will see them in water having a warmer temperature than other bodies of water. They can be found on a regular basis in the back of Gainesville Creek during colder periods. They also can be seen in the back of Flat Creek.

Can you use your "Herring" net to catch Gizzard Shad? Yes; however there are some considerations you should understand. First, a net with a one inch mesh and more weight would be better suited to catch Gizzards. Ideally, the net for catching Gizzards wouldhave a significant sinking rate and you can obtain that rate with a larger mesh and more weight on the radius. Gizzards can sometimes be seen "flipping" which is to say that you can see their tail fin on the surface of the water. When you cannot see them, concentrate in the backs of creeks in which the water is slightly stained. There is a fair number of Gizzards in the river channel and small coves just off the river channel north of Clarks Bridge.

When catching bait with your net, you should initially place the bait in a large, water-filled bucket in which they will defecate and regurgitate. Allow them this opportunity prior to placing any bait in your bait tank.

The Blueback Herring

Blueback Herring: No, you are not going to receive information here on Latin terms describing the Blueback; but what is important is information that will help you catch Stripers. First, a Blueback can reach a maximum size of sixteen inches and weight of seven ounces; it can live up to eight years. Okay—please give me your undivided attention. When water temperatures reach 70 degrees F, Bluebacks begin their spawn. The Bluebacks spawn in late March to mid-May and a female five years and older will deposit between 60,000 and 100,000 eggs on hard objects like gravel, riprap, rocks, wood, seawall, etc. These two small facts will help you catch stripers!

During this period you should use your Planer Boards and Flat-Lines. You can, and should pull your outside planer board right on the bank! That's right, bounce your board off the rocks if you can. Now you understand why—there are thousands of Herring on structure near or on the banks. So, that's why your outside planer board will always catch fish! After spawning, the Herring move away from the bank and Wham!—Your inside planer board dives three feet underwater! Fish On!

For readers who have never seen a Blueback Herring go to your local live bait purveyor and ask to see one.

The Blueback has proven to be a major source of food for Lanier Striper and it is widely known that Striper growth rates have increased due to the addition of the Blueback to the Stripers' menu. The Striper and the Blueback have one thing in common that is important to understand—they are both comfortable living in colder water temperatures. On the other hand, Threadfin Shad are not comfortable in colder water. More on that later.

Blueback Herring eat microscopic plants and plankton, small insects, small fish and fish eggs. As stated earlier, Bluebacks are attracted to light and during certain periods will come to the surface when the sun is shining; on the other hand, they tend to go deep on overcast days.

Gizzard Shad

Gizzard Shad: The choice bait for Striper Fishermen seeking a trophy fish. The average size is ten to twelve inches and the maximum weight is two pounds. Gizzards like warm and shallow bodies of water with soft mud bottoms and a little silt in the water. Water temperature plays an important role in the life of a Gizzard; between 38 degrees F. and 57 degrees F., Gizzards are somewhat inactive. Below 38 degrees F., Gizzards may die. On Lanier, Gizzards are more prevalent in the backs of stained creeks including Flat Creek and those creeks north of Browns Bridge.

The diet of a Gizzard Shad changes during its lifetime. They initially feed on zooplankton using their teeth to catch them. However, when they reach one inch in length, they lose their teeth and become filter feeders, consuming both small invertebrates and phytoplankton.

Gizzards spawn in protected shallow water coves and backwaters along the shoreline and near the surface in water between one to three feet deep. Eggs sink to the bottom and drift in the current (when available) and will adhere to submerged vegetation, rocks, or any objects they come in contact with. Spawning takes place between late March and late June but peaks with water temperatures of 66 degrees F. to 70 degrees F. Younger female Gizzards can produce 380,000 to 400,000 eggs while egg production of older females will drop to about 12,500. Spawning activity is greatest in the evening and early night and declines during daylight hours. Females are accompanied by several males during the spawning process. One other thing—females are more abundant than males because males experience a more extensive post-spawning mortality rate. Remember them as another example of a bait fish that should be in shallow water during the spring and another reason to use your Planer Boards and Flat-Lines in shallow water.

Threadfin Shad

Threadfin Shad: These are the bait fish you see early in the morning and late afternoon on the surface. One of the reasons they are on the surface is that they are eating plankton that is sensitive to light. As you probably know, the lake is full of Threadfins. An adult Threadfin would measure five to seven inches; however the predominate size is one to two inches. The Threadfins do not like cold water temperatures. As a matter of fact, some will die when the water temperature reaches 45 degrees F. The bottom line is that they cannot survive in water with a temperature of 35 degrees F. or less. Again, this should be helpful when fishing for Stripers—recognizing that a species of baitfish will seek warm water of at least 45 degrees F. or greater in the winter.

When water temperatures reach the high sixties, look for females to lay eggs on hard surfaces in shallow water; males will fertilize the eggs from morning twilight to sunrise. For the most part, Threadfins stay in open deep water until there is a change in the water temperature.

It seems that every winter there will be a time in which the Stripers focus almost solely on the Threadfin. For this reason, it would be wise to have available your cast net, small hooks, and eight-pound leader material. There are instances on Lanier like this that would be classified as "counter-intuitive"—why would an eighteen pound Striper want to eat a two inch Threadfin? While all this may not seem to make any sense at first, it does pay to be attentive and in sync with the current fishing conditions.

While Blueback Herring, Gizzard Shad, Threadfin Shad, Shiners, and Spot Tail minnows live in the Lake and may be taken legally by a cast net, there is one species that is used for bait and they can be purchased locally. One of the favorite baits for Stripers on Lanier is trout.

Trout

Trout: From late summer to early summer, Trout are very popular. They may be fished on down-lines, planer boards, and flat-lines. Like small Threadfins, Stripers will sometimes target only small Trout. Be sure to let your local Bait Shop know what size Trout appeals to the Stripers. Trout seem to have a supply of never-ending energy, which they use to swim up, down, and all around. They are constantly tugging on the rod tip. Stripers love them. You cannot go wrong with Trout for Striper bait.

Bream

Bream: While Bream caught with a cast net may not be legally used for bait, those hooked with rod/reel currently qualify under Georgia State rules. There are several features of the Bream that appeal to most Striper fishermen. First, Bream are hearty and flexible with respect to warm water temperatures. Bream may be caught around docks and ramps using crickets and worms. I have to admit that catching them is a source of fun. Stripers will readily take a Bream; of course, they will always attempt to take a Bream head first. So, it sometimes pays to be a little patient with a feeding Striper that is working one of them. Remember that the Striper is attempting to get the Bream in a head-first position! I find Bream to be excellent bait especially in late spring and early summer; they can be rather lethargic in cooler waters. For this reason, you should consider using Bream on Planer boards and Flat-lines during and after their breeding season.

Keeping your bait lively

Maintaining bait begins with your onboard tank(s). Remember that a clean tank is a happy tank. Some boats have one or more built-in tanks which may be of different sizes and constructed with or without insulation. Some have a built-in pump and an aeration system while some will not. Bait tanks come in different configurations- oval versus round; so when discussing them, these variables need to be considered. Periodically clean the bait tank. This can be accomplished with a damp towel. Wipe the inside of the tank and the lid. Remove the filtration system and rinse or replace the charcoal. Replace the material you are using to catch scales. On an infrequent basis, you should consider using a mild detergent to clean all internal components of the tank, including the hose. The final step includes a thorough rinsing of both the outside and inside of the tank.

Water quality is a major consideration when fishing with bait. The temperature in your tank should be around 65 degrees F. If you are using the water from a bait shop, take the time to determine the temperature. Late spring, summer, and early fall sometimes have excessively hot days that tend to warm the bait tank water resulting in dead or lethargic bait. Pinpoint currently makes a wireless product that consists of a temperature sensor/transmitter and a receiver which will provide the water temperature of the bait tank in a real time fashion. Mount the receiver within eyesight or simply place it in a convenient place. Otherwise, use a thermometer to monitor the temperature.

In the event the water temperature increases, you can either add ice or containers having ice in them. Be careful not to lower the temperature too quickly because this will shock or kill the bait. Some ice contains chemicals such as chlorine which will have a detrimental effect on the bait while other ice is produced without bait damaging chemicals (for example Reddy Ice).

There are some products sold at retail stores and bait shops which will help keep your bait healthy. Bait Saver is a product that when used properly helps coat scale-damaged areas and it eliminates chlorine and other trace chemical/metals. The rule of thumb is to add one teaspoon for every twenty five gallons of water.

Before you transfer bait such as Herring from the tank at the bait store to your tank you should add rock salt to your tank. Rock salt ranks as one of the most important chemical additives. It will offset the effect of the defecation/regurgitation; will assist in the maintenance of the slime coat over the baits' skin; and it helps to bond the scales of the baitfish. One cup to every ten gallons should do it. Do not use iodized salt.

Rock salt and Bait Saver should be added prior to placing the baitfish in your tank.

Keep an eye on your Bait! The captain or a crew member must monitor the bait on a frequent basis. Monitor the water temperature and clarity; examine the baitfish for red nose (Herring and Shad) or black backs (Herring); remove all dead and nearly dead baitfish immediately. The captain and crew must also monitor the presence of foam on top of the water.

Foam is caused by ammonia which is the result of waste expelled from the baitfish. This situation cannot be treated lightly and it must be remedied as soon as possible because foam prevents carbon dioxide from leaving the water. Purchase and use Foam Off or a similar product. A few drops of Foam Off will disseminate the foam. Unfortunately, your bait tank water still has some carbon dioxide in it so be diligent and continue to monitor this. Should foam reappear, consider changing the water.

Bait tips:

· *When purchasing bait, ask the attendant to transport no more than two dozen baits per five gallon bucket unless your bucket has a bubbler.*

· *Do not add uncured Gizzard Shad (recently caught) to a tank containing Herring.*

- *When your bait-tank water temperature needs to be reduced, do not reduce it more than three degrees F. per minute.*

- *When fishing with Herring in the summer, do your best to send the Herring and your terminal tackle to a prescribed depth as quickly as possible.*

- *Where possible, do not use Herring with red-nose or black backs.*

- *Usually, the healthiest Herring are located in the bottom of your bait tank.*

- *Limit the number of baits to two baits per gallon of water in your bait tank.*

The latest and greatest in bait tank technology

The latest technology regarding bait maintenance is aerating with portable oxygen. That's right. The oxygen system for bait maintenance consists of a bottle of oxygen, tubing, regulator, and a diffuser. It's simple and inexpensive and it has many advantages over the bait maintenance system consisting of pumps, power bubbler systems, filters, etc.

Adoption of the oxygen system will result in improvements. The first big change I saw was the increased strength and vitality of the Herring. When releasing my down-line with a two ounce sinker, the Herring would literally drag the sinker away from the boat. At the end of a full day of fishing, I noticed very few scales in the bottom of the bait tank. Of course, this is a major consideration because one of the bait killing items in a tank is fish scales. The oxygen that is forced into the tank helps to cool it and that's a welcome change from the power bubble system which is forcing ambient air into the tank. The oxygen tank does not require power from the battery and does not cause electrical interference with your electronics.

In conclusion, can bait be maintained with only filters, pumps, and aerators? Absolutely. Does oxygen compare favorably with the yesterday's technology? Examine your budget and, if possible, acquire the oxygen system if you think it can be carried and used safely on your boat.

IV
Considerations and Planning

Lake Lanier Striper fisherman need to rethink how a fishing season should be defined. For years, we have discussed seasons in a traditional fashion: trolling season, planer board season, etc. Maybe it is time to debunk this mindset and adopt a new set of criteria that will take you over the edge.

Folks, I say it's time to think outside of the box. We have learned one important fact and that is bait movement, bait habitat, and therefore Striper activity may be directly linked to water temperature. Therefore, our focus should be water temperature!

Let's use a water temperature chart to identify bait and Striper activity and link that information with a fish catching strategy. Isn't it better to predict where the fish are going to be instead of hearing from your buddies where they were a little while ago?

Water temperature range: 30 F to 40 F. There would be no Threadfin shad in water with this temperature range; nor would there be any Gizzards considering they can die when the water temperature reaches 38 F. Herring and Stripers forced to live in this water would be at best lethargic. Fishing strategy: Seek warmer water temperatures.

Water temperature range: 40 F to 50 F. While you could expect to find Gizzard Shad in this range, they would be somewhat inactive. Threadfins sometimes die when the temperature is 45 F; therefore, you can expect some of them to die while others will be very inactive. In the low 40s Herring and Stripers would be somewhat inactive; however, in the upper 40s you can expect Herring, Gizzards and Stripers to be active. Fishing strategy: Acquire Gizzards and Trout and place them on Planer Boards and Flat-lines. Regardless of whether you see Stripers roiling on the surface, throw a fluke or small Bucktail Jig while moving the boat. At this temperature, you can expect Stripers to "pick-off" dying or weak Threadfins. If your Gizzards and Trout do not produce in an hour or two, throw your cast net on some Threadfins and use them.

Water temperature range: 50 F to 60 F. Oh Boy! Now we're talking about trophy Stripers. Virtually all of the baitfish as well as the Stripers will be active in this range. Stripers are very comfortable in this range and we believe that the largest ones are most comfortable at 53 F. Your strategy should be to find water in this temperature range with a fair amount of bait. Assuming you will target a trophy fish; acquire some large bait including Gizzards and Trout. If you think some of your baits are too big, remember this motto: "it's not big enough". If you are after big fish, use big bait.

Planer Boards, Flat-lines, and Down-lines will be effective. Don't leave home without your Umbrella Rigs. Throw artificial lures including small Bucktail Jigs, Flukes, and Jerk Baits.

Water temperature range: 60 F to 70 F. All of the bait-fish described in this text will be very active. As you may recall, Threadfins, Gizzards, and Herring will be spawning in this range. Pull Planer Boards on the bank because that big Striper will be targeting the spawning bait. Be sure to use your Flat-lines and Down-lines. Your Umbrella Rigs will be effective. Throwing artificial lures will be effective also.

Water temperature range: 70 F to 80 F. Yes, some baitfish will spawn in the lower 70s. Gizzards, Herring, and Threadfins are active in this water temperature range. In the lower 70s, you may pull Planer Boards and Flat-lines; however, Trout are unhappy in water temps above 68. If you like to use Trout, put them on a Down-line. As the water temperature approaches 80, the Herring, if they could talk, would tell you they do not like water that warm. They would be happy on a Down-line. By the time most of the Lake is reporting 80, you will be Down-lining and trolling with your Umbrella Rigs.

Water temperature range: 80 F and above. I hope you have some Lead-Core and Down-Rigger lines because these two techniques are very popular. Down-lining the

Bluebacks is extremely popular. And every year it seems that more and more Striper fishermen can catch fish with Umbrella Rigs when water is warm. Fishermen with artificials will be successful using Jigs, Spoons, and Swim Baits. Threadfins and Gizzards will enjoy water in this temperature range while the Blueback Herring will seek water with temperatures in the low 70s and upper 60s. It is to your advantage to fish beneath the warmer water.

A little bit about the Weather

Weather is the current state of the atmosphere and the status of the atmosphere as time passes. Weather consists of elements such as wind, cloud formations, atmospheric pressure, etc., which are the results of "fronts". What is happening with the weather will almost always affect your fishing in some way or the other.

For our purposes, there are two kinds of fronts: a cold front and a warm front. Let's look at each and relate the characteristics to striper fishing.

Cold Fronts

A cold front is defined as the leading edge of a cooler and drier mass of air which is replacing a warmer mass of air located at ground level. Here is a general description of each stage of a cold front.

A cold front has these characteristics: Cooler and denser air; replaces warm air; usually associated with an area of low pressure; usually fast moving.

Prior to the passage of the Front, you will experience warm temperatures, a steadily decreasing barometric pressure and a change in wind direction.

As the cold front passes you should see a rather sudden change in temperature; barometric pressure will be very low; gusty and shifting winds accompanied by a sudden drop in the dew point; and the possibility of thunderstorms.

After the cold front has passed look for steadily cooling temperatures; barometric pressure steadily increasing; a wind direction shift from east or north to west; showers followed by clearing skies and a falling dew point.

As a cold front approaches, the barometric pressure decreases. The barometric pressure is the weight of the atmosphere measured by a barometric gauge. Should you be fishing on the day in which the cold front is approaching and the barometric pressure is going down? Absolutely. It's during this period that fishing can be at its best.

Barometric pressure can range from 29 inches (usually very poor weather conditions) to 31 inches (excellent weather). A range from 29 to 31 inches is small. For that reason you should be attentive to small changes to the pressure. A quality onboard barometric gauge is a must! They are inexpensive and provide useful information. You should maintain a fishing journal or a software program that will assist you in recording pressures (and related changes).

Warm Fronts

Prior to the arrival of a warm front, winds will be south or southwest; temperatures will be cool but there will be some evidence of a slow warming; the barometric pressure will usually fall; and the dew point will show a steady rise.

As the warm front passes, winds become light and variable; there will be a steady rise in the temperature and the barometric pressure will level off. The dew point will be steady.

After the warm front passes, winds will remain south to southwest; temperatures will become warmer—then become steady. The barometric pressure will rise slightly and then fall. The dew point will rise slightly and then rise.

Barometric Pressure and Wind

A general rule is that the fishing is very good when the barometric pressure is dropping. Many times a smidgen of a decrease can ignite the urge for a Striper to start feeding. So, in consideration of this, do your best to get on the lake just prior to the arrival of a warm front. As the warm front weakens and begins to pass, you will have another opportunity to fish a decreasing barometric pressure.

Not every fisherman can fish that specific day and time in which the barometric pressure is falling; however, there will always be other days in which the fishing is above average or better. Those days occur when a stable weather pattern is in place. More specifically, on the third and sometimes second day of a stable weather pattern, fishing can be superb. Our journals indicate that Stripers become active as the front approaches, become rather inactive during the first day or so of the arrival of the front, and then become active on those days when the pattern is stable.

Everyone learns from their fishing experiences while on Lanier. It's wise to document your fishing experiences and nothing helps you more than time on the water.

Certain elements of weather affect everyone. Some of us do not fare well when temperatures are excessively cold and/or hot. Many fishermen will stay home on days in which gusty winds are in the forecast. A number of fishermen will not fish in the rain. Gosh, how will some of you get your time-on-the-water experiences if you are a bluebird fisherman? As you can see, certain elements of weather strip us of our desire to go fishing even on those days in which the Stripers should be active.

While we are not suggesting that you go fishing in an ice storm, it has to be stressed that fishing can be very good when weather conditions are not the best. Remember, weather and fishing conditions can improve in a matter of hours.

Does wind affect your decision to go fishing? What wind direction is your favorite? Have you been successful under gusty wind conditions? Wind is an element of weather that definitely affects both the fisherman and the Stripers.

Wind has an effect on the food chain by moving plankton and other related organisms; small bait fish feed on the plankton; and predators such as the Striper follow. Over a period of several days in which the wind direction is the same, fishermen should look for bait and fish on points, land, and shallow underwater bars that are receiving the wind. Fishermen should also be attentive to wind changes. Here is an oldie but goodie, "Wind from the south blows the hook in the fish's mouth". Carefully kept journals of fishing indicate that such a wind change can result in an increase in Striper feeding activity.

In addition to weather changes from the passing of fronts, the impact of barometric pressure changes, and the effects of the wind, the Sun plays a major role in the life of a Striper fisherman. Sometimes sunlight is desirable and other times not. Fishermen using down-line and trolling techniques usually see sunlight as an advantage while those using Planer board and Flat line fishing would prefer less light.

Lake Stratification and Turnover

The sun plays another very significant role as it is solely responsible for the stratification of a fresh water impoundment like Lake Lanier. The stratification process is central to developing your fishing strategy; knowing the temperatures and depths of the various layers of water represent the foundation of a successful day on the Lake.

Longer days are a part of spring and summer and with the Sun and accompanying heat, water on Lanier begins to warm. This warming process causes the lake to stratify. Three layers will form; the Epilimnion or top layer; the Thermocline which is the middle layer; and the Hypolimion or bottom layer. By mid-summer, the Thermocline has fully formed. At this time, the top layer lacks adequate amounts of oxygen to sustain Stripers on a routine basis; on the other hand, the Thermocline has two attributes favorable to Stripers—oxygenated water and cooler temperatures. Many times your sonar unit will display the thermocline. Blueback Herring will seek the Thermocline as well thus making it that much more desirable for the Stripers to live in this layer.

With the Lake stratification in place, Striper fishermen will use four methods of fishing: Lead-core trolling; Down Lines; Down-rigger trolling; and artificial (jigging & casting). When surface temperatures reach the mid to high 80s, you will find fish as deep as 100 feet. These methods and related conditions are discussed later in the book.

In late summer and autumn there is a weather change. As a result of diminishing hours of sunlight and the occurrence of cold air masses, the temperature of the upper layers eventually becomes cooler. Cooler water becomes denser and thus heavier than the layer below it. When this occurs, the cooler water will sink resulting in the displacement of the water in the lower layers. This is called "Lake Turnover".

So now, the water from the Thermocline and the Hypolimion circulate upward from their depths. This can be evidenced by the release of sulphurous gases and the related rotten-egg odor. The released gases will show as slanted lines on your sonar unit. Drive over the dam and you will see the pea-green color of the released water.

The fall Lake Turnover does not occur simultaneously across the entire Lake and you can count on a Turnover period of seven to ten weeks. Fishing during the Turnover is tough because the fishing pattern is very inconsistent.

Use your knowledge of weather fronts, barometric pressure, the effects of wind, and Lake stratification/turnover to assist in forming a strategy for finding and catching Stripers.

The thing to remember is that Stripers, like you, seek out places and conditions where they feel comfortable and can find something to eat. So study the previous pages carefully and set in your mind how that comfort zone changes seasonally. If you do, you are well on your way to finding more fish.

V
Putting it all Together

Now it's time to do something with all of this new information. After all, you want to catch more fish. Right? So let's get at it.

The next sections will discuss everything you will need to know to get on the water and fish for striper from the basics to more advanced techniques. To begin this section, a brief discussion of bait is in order, however, it is impossible to not use some terminology that will be covered in depth in the following pages, so bear with it. It will all come together soon.

Selecting and Fishing your Bait

There's no question that live bait is heavily used year-round by Striper fishermen. Because all bait fish react differently to water temperature and other conditions, it would be wise to identify the favorite bait fish species and their related nuances. In previous sections, we learned about various types of live bait. Now it's time to discuss what to do with it.

Blueback Herring

Blueback Herring are permanent residents of Lanier and by far the most widely used bait. In fall, winter, and spring, they may be fished on Planer Boards, Flat-lines, and Down-lines. Once the surface temperatures reach 80 F, Bluebacks should not be used on the surface. Bluebacks are the favorite bait for cut-bait fishermen.

Under certain circumstances, they may be pitched to Stripers feeding on the surface or on points, rocks, and shallow bars. In the summer, Blueback prefer cooler water which of course fits perfectly with your plan to use them on Down-lines. While they would prefer to be dropped to the Thermocline, anglers routinely suspend them at 40 to 100 feet with great success.

Gizzard Shad

Big Gizzards are a favorite with trophy striper fishermen and are most effective on Planer Boards and Flat-lines in the fall, winter, and spring. Remember that they are susceptible to cold water temperatures. Depending on the size, be prepared to use a stinger hook.

Trout

Trout are purchased from bait stores. (It is illegal to catch them by hook and then use them on Lanier for bait). Striper fishermen love to use Trout for bait, whether on Planer Boards, Flat-lines, or Down-lines because they seem to be very active while hooked, which will draw the attention of a Striper. They perform best when used in water temperatures 70 F or less. The good news is that both large and medium sized Trout are sold and each size has its own purpose. There are times on Lanier when Stripers will shy away from large baits regardless of the water depth—this is where the medium sized Trout meets the demand. Again, a Trout is very hearty and can stay on your line for a long period of time. The large Trout are excellent for targeting big Stripers when river fishing. Larger Trout may require a stinger hook.

Shiners

Have you ever fished the same Shiner all day? There's a time and place for Shiners. They do well in your bait tank, on the line, and attracting Stripers. They can be fished as a surface-bait or on a Down-line. They perform well in a wide range of water temperature 50 F. to 80 F.

Threadfin Shad

Threadfins are less durable than most bait on Lanier and therefore require a significant amount of "hand holding". Be sure your bait tank and water are both set up perfectly.

From small to trophy–sized Stripers, Threadfins will deliver. They will provide the knock-out punch whether used on Down-lines, Planer Boards, or Flat Lines. Due to their size and vulnerability to adverse conditions, we suggest that you check Threadfins more frequently than you would with other bait species. Put fresh Threadfins on your line more frequently. Remember to place them in a bucket prior to dumping them in your bait tank. Throw some rock salt in your tank prior to the Threadfins.

Bream

Bream are a durable bait and comfortable in water temperatures of 70 to 84 degrees F. Bream (some folks call them Sunfish) must be caught with a reel/rod to be considered legal bait on Lake Lanier. The best application for Bream is a surface-bait either pulled behind a Planer Board or attached to a flat line.

Selecting your line, leader & hook

Line

Most of the time your base line should be high quality 20 pound test monofilament line. Base line plays a major role in your Herring when Flat-line and Planer Board fishing. For example, 40 pound test line is heavier, stiffer, and larger diameter than 20 pound test. This additional weight will have a detrimental effect on smaller live bait by not letting it swim naturally, even if you use a lighter leader. It is also possible that your reel may not handle heavy line well. Match your reel to the line weight you select.

By the way, change your line every once in a while. Old line takes on a set from being on the reel, and will not lay properly in the water. You will lose fish if you use old line.

Leader

For the most part, the water in Lanier is fairly clear; thus, the need for a fluorocarbon leader. Most fishermen whether live or cut-bait fishing will use this technique. Leader length may vary; for down line and flat line fishing, the general rule is five to nine feet. This can vary depending on personal preference but it is good to start in this range of length. Anything longer than nine feet will probably not give you any additional advantage.

Once you have decided on the brand of fluorocarbon, you should decide its strength, i.e. fourteen or seventeen pounds. You may have some twelve pound handy too. There are times when the bite is light and you are using small bait. In these instances, 12 pound leader is handy to use, however you will run the risk of breaking off large fish if you are not careful.

Hook

Here is a very important point. If you plan to use Blueback Herring that are five inches long, you have to decide on the proper hook size as well.

First, lay the Blueback Herring and a hook on any surface to determine whether the hook is too big. An excessively large hook will quickly cause Herring fatigue and premature death; the same can be said for too heavy of a fluorocarbon or monofilament leader.

Judge the hook size requirement as a function of the bait size not the size of the fish you are pursuing. Let's go one step further to make the point very clear—the fish that you are pursuing should determine the size of the bait.

Generally, you can use a size 1 or 1/0 circle hook for the average-sized Herring. Leader strength will vary from 12 to 17 pounds. The general rule on Lanier is that the leader with less strength will result in more bites.

Do not mix used hooks with new hooks as any rust from the old hooks may infect the new ones.

Remember that there is a tendency on the part of live bait (especially a Blueback) to foul hook itself. To reduce the possibility of this, consider placing a small piece of rubber band or tie a small knot in the bend of the hook.

Down Lining Live Baits

What is this that we cannot live without? It's Down Line Fishing. It ranks with Planer Board Fishing as the top addiction on Lake Lanier. The beauty of the down line technique is that is can be used successfully every day of the year. Equipment requirements are minimal. However, it does require a few things of the average fisherman.

The two important aspects of Down Line fishing consist of: the proper presentation of bait and the ability of the Captain to maintain depth control. We have discussed the importance of bait maintenance in a previous chapter.

Depth Control—Equipment: To be successful with down lines, the bait must be placed above the Stripers. This is called depth control. There are tools which will assist you in this process. First, it would be wise to use line-counter reels; terminal tackle should include a weight (sinker); and your trolling motor speed must be controlled.

As discussed previously, it's wise to begin with a line-counter reel, a seven and one-half ft. Shakespeare Ugly Stick, 20 pound line on the reel, a two-ounce sinker, a fluorocarbon leader 12lb to 17lb, and a circle/octopus hook.

The advantage of a line counter reel is that you always know the depth of every rig on the boat; it's a given that while fishing over trees, you will adjust the depth of each rig both up and down to place your bait at the optimum depth and to avoid an entanglement with gear-robbing structure. Accordingly, a line counter reel provides assurance that every rig is exactly at the optimal depth. As the depth of the Stripers change, the depth of your terminal tackle may be changed quickly and accurately with the use of a line counter reel.

To reach the ultimate level of accuracy, line counter reels need to have the maximum amount of line prescribed by the manufacturer.

Hook sizes, of course, will vary by the size of the bait. While a size six hook may be just right for Shiners, a 4/0 would be best for medium Trout. A size one or 1/0 would be perfect for the average sized Herring. Matching the hook size with the size of the bait cannot be over emphasized.

Invariably, one question frequently asked is, "Should the rod be held or placed in a rod holder?" If a survey were to be conducted, the results would show that the best hook-up ratio occurs when the rod is placed in the rod holder. This assumes you are using either a circle or octopus hook which, as we have learned, is designed to "self hook" the Striper. In this example, to hold the rod and attempt to set the hook is self-defeating and will result in fewer fish to the boat. If your preference is to hold the rod, consider changing the style of the hook.

Depth Control—Sinkers. Targeting and searching for Stripers is fun and challenging but, once you have found them, you must engage them. As an example: Your sonar unit is reporting fish in the range of 35ft to 80ft. This would indicate fishing during the summer months. The favorite summer bait is Herring and you know it is important to place the Herring at depths where water temperature is in the mid seventies or lower. The tool that accomplishes this goal is the sinker—generally two ounces. A sinker with a swivel at each end is recommended. With the sinker on the surface and your Herring in the water, "zero-out" your line counter reel and allow the sinker and bait to drop to the desired depth.

Depth Control—Trolling Motor. Most fishermen will engage their electric trolling motor while down line fishing. Again, your goal is to keep your baits in a specified depth range. Depending on the weight of the sinkers, you may or may not be able to consistently maintain the prescribed depth. On the average, a two-ounce sinker (preferably painted red) will allow your Carolina rig to stay in the targeted range with a trolling speed of .60 mph to .75 mph. To move the boat faster than this range is to lose depth control and to do so consistently without adjusting for the additional speed will result in less success.

Like most fishing techniques, there is no hard and fast rule about using your trolling motor to move the boat. Generally, there is a breeze on the Lake and without a trolling motor your boat will be subjected to the strength and direction of the wind. So, if for no other purpose, a trolling motor allows the captain to position his boat over fish, to establish a course on which he believes the fish are moving, and to maintain a safe distance from other boats. All of these functions may be successfully performed with the use of a remote controlled trolling motor.

The remote can be used from anywhere on the boat; but most importantly, the captain can monitor the movement of the boat and the location of the fish while at the helm. Without question, the trolling motor is an integral part of the down line fishing process and when used properly will assist the fisherman in keeping live bait in the strike zone.

Leaders should consist of fluorocarbon material; their length will vary by the nature of your fishing method. In the clear waters of the Lake, a Striper will use his keen eyesight to potentially spot all or portions of your terminal tackle. While you may not be able to completely disguise the tackle, consider using fluorocarbon of 12 to 17 pounds for down-lined leaders. Fluorocarbon leader material from Suffix, Bass Pro Shop or Gamma will provide strength and an ability to withstand abusive underwater structure. Because it is virtually invisible to his eye, fluorocarbon will make it almost impossible for that trophy to see your leader.

When fishing in stained water with a depth range of zero to 50 feet, use leaders four to six feet. On the other hand, down line fishing in the crystal-clear summer waters will require longer leaders—6 to 9 feet.

There are various ways in which to "hook your bait". First, you can place the hook in the upper lip by bringing the hook from the mouth through the upper lip. This method will reduce the possibility that your bait will become foul hooked. Assuming you intend to place your hook through the nostrils, you should consider placing a small obstruction on the hook to keep the bait from foul hooking itself like placing a small piece of rubber band on the hook; this should meet your objective.

When using small baits such as Threadfins and Shiners, it will be difficult to place the hook through the upper limit and you may be forced to either use the "through-the-nostril "or "both lip" method. You should not encounter any problems with Trout or Gizzard Shad. For those of you not completely satisfied with a hook in the mouth or nostrils, there is always the hook behind the dorsal fin or the hook in the meat just ahead of the tail fin. Neither one of these methods would qualify as my favorite because a bait with an embedded hook is a bait with a shortened life.

Depth Control—Sonar Unit. As discussed previously, one of the keys to successful Striper fishing is the application of your experience and knowledge to your equipment which, in the case of down line fishing, is your sonar unit. Not only will you be required to correctly identify stripers on the unit, but you will also be challenged by how to best use the unit. When properly used, you will be able to identify the individual fish in a school and their respective depths. Apply this information to your depth counter reels taking into consideration that the physical attributes of a Striper allow them to look vertically up and horizontally— but not vertically down. Accordingly, keep the bait above the fish!

Upon finding fish you should use your waypoint function to establish where you first began marking them and continue this process as you make way on the water. This technique will provide a trail marked with waypoints where fish were seen and may assist in determining the direction of the school(s). The general rule to remember here—especially for summertime fishing—is that Stripers will move from shallow areas to deeper waters as the morning progresses. In the winter months, Stripers will generally move from the shallower backs of creeks into deeper areas of the creek during the morning hours.

Once you have established a successful pattern, use it during the day. Example: if you have found and caught fish about half-way back in a south end creek in 60 to 70 feet of water depth in the early afternoon with a water temperature of 80 degrees F., take this information and apply it to other creeks that same day. This should be the primary source of information when establishing your search pattern.

Stripers may be found in the deeper depths of Lanier, especially during warmer water temperatures; therefore, be sure that your sonar unit will report the entire water column.

Once you have achieved success and you have the fish aboard, there are some issues to be considered. Whenever possible, do not use a net to land the fish. The net will remove the protective slime from the skin. If you are going to place the fish on a surface, wet it first. Be quick with all of your actions such as picture taking, weighing, measuring, etc. Remember that a fish out of the water is without oxygen.

Fish are very susceptible to harm and damage in the summertime. The best method for releasing a fish caught in the summer is the torpedo method where it is shoved head first into the water. Again, minimize the time out of the water and reduce any contact with any surface material on the boat. Use a wet towel where possible.

Planer board & Flat-line fishing equipment, hook size, leaders, knots & split shot

Planer board and flat line fishing represent the most exciting form of fishing on Lanier. This top water technique can result in some explosive Striper action that many folks liken to the sound of a cinder block falling in the water.

While Stripers have an aversion to light, they none-theless seek bait located in the top twenty to thirty feet of the water column. From mid October to mid June, virtually all Lanier fishermen gear-up for live bait fishing with Planer boards and Flat lines.

Ramping up for this type of fishing requires planer boards, rods and reels as previously described, floats, and of course hooks, line, leader, and sometimes lead weights. Rigging a rod and reel for planer boards and flat lines will require at least 20 pound test line on the reel, a bead, a swivel, 12 to 17 pound leader, and a hook.

The Planer Board's purpose is to take your line with an attached live bait or artificial lure to a particular side of the boat and to some measurable distance away from the boat. While some fishermen utilize four or more boards on each side of the boat, most folks on Lanier will only place two to three. Some fishermen believe that a boat will spook fish that are in shallow water or engaged in a shallow feeding pattern; therefore, the placement of lines on the sides of the boat is called for. The use of the boards allows a fisher-man to cover a lot of water with baits.

Planer boards come in different sizes ranging from six to about 18 inches. Wind velocity and wave action dictate planer board size. The Planer Board should be painted a color which may be easily seen from a distance. In the event your board "kicks off", you want to be able to see it. Some fishermen write contact information on the board in the event of loss. Depending on the type and manufacturer of the board, it will have a release and in most cases a snap swivel or pin through which the line will pass. The purpose of the bead is to catch the snap swivel and prevent the board from floating back to that 25 pounder that is on the end of your line!

Some boards have an adjustable release. Take a look at your boards to determine whether the release is equipped with an embedded tension spring. Tension on the spring is adjusted by moving the spring. Moving it forward increases the tension. By setting the spring completely forward it will provide maximum tension on the release. Less tension sometimes causes the board to break free when larger than average waves are present or when you are about to set the board at its desired location and accidentally pull the rod to the holder with a quick jerking action.

Think about using flash adhesive sheets on the metal or wood part of your planer boards. The purpose of the "flash" is to draw the attention of a Striper and to get it to look up. In some cases, the flash may look like a large bait fish. Now, with an attentive and inquisitive fish looking up, your live bait passes over him and BAM—you got a hook-up!

Generally a release is attached to a Board with a split ring; you can avoid a major line entanglement by placing a barrel swivel between the release and the split ring.

Okay, let's put out the planer boards. You have determined that you are going to use Herring for bait and your trolling speed will be approximately 0.8 mph. How much line you place behind the first board depends on these and other related conditions. If you wish to pull the outside board on or very near the bank and the depth of the water next to the bank is 10 feet, you may want to have about five to ten feet behind the board. At this point, place the line in the release and the snap swivel and put it over the side. Monitor the total amount of line released and the board's location in relation to the bank. Once you are satisfied with this board's location, you are ready for board number two. Place the baited line overboard and closely monitor the amount of line you release from the reel. Consider placing the board on the line after releasing approximately 35 feet. Repeat this process on the opposite side of the boat.

At the end of this exercise, the "outside" board is the first to be placed overboard while the second line will be labeled your "inside" line. If you have never "pulled" Planer boards, you should practice this with or without bait. Once you have the boards under control, it's time to engage the Flat lines.

Complimenting the boards with Flat lines should be a big part of your top-water strategy. As its name implies, a Flat line is a line released with live bait that may or may not be weighted. It consists of a rod/reel, twenty pound test line on the reel, a bead, a barrel swivel, six to nine feet fluorocarbon leader, and a hook. While a bead is not needed for a Flat line, it should be added so that the rod/reel may also be used as a Planer board line if needed. If pulling boards and flat lines is "new" to you, you should limit your rig to just one Flat line.

Once you feel comfortable with the boards and possibly one flat line, take the next step by setting two Flat lines. Set up one with large bait such as a Gizzard Shad or Trout approximately 100 feet behind the boat and a second flat line approximately 50 feet with average sized bait.

You don't need to have a degree in math or physics to determine that there is a likelihood one or more of the lines may cross while making a turn. No, let's rephrase that—they will cross—it's just a matter of time.

What can you do to avoid crossing the lines? First, make wide sweeping turns when the conditions allow it. Second, do not allow the line from the outside board to contact the inside board. The lines and related boards running on the side of the boat which will be on the inside of the turn will provide the biggest challenge. One preventive measure is to slowly place some line back on the reel related to the inside board—bring it in closer to the boat during the turn. This should help greatly. After making the turn, release more line allowing the board to regain its prior position.

Our discussion now turns back to the rod mounting locations mentioned in the earlier parts of this book. If you own a boat with a T-Top, mount rod holders on the side of the Top. The rod with the inside board should be placed in the rod holder located closer to the bow while the rod with the outside board should be placed in the rod holder closer to the stern. The rocket launchers on the back of the T-Top may be used for flat line fishing, provided you use a float or other similar device, like a balloon. The float provides accurate depth control.

You do not need a T-Top to properly mount your rod holders. However, you should consider three very important issues: one, the rod holder closest to the bow should hold the rod with the inside board while the rod holder closest to the stern should hold the outside board; second, the line from your rod tips to the boards should be completely out of the water except when making sharp turns, third, if space permits, the rod holders should allow the rods to be mounted in such a manner that the rod tips will be at a 45 degree angle (or greater) to the water level. The higher the rod tip, the more flexibility you will have with the placement of the board.

You can control the depth of the baits on Planer Boards and Flat lines using one or a combination of three methods: first, the trolling motor speed plays a major part in the depth of the baits—more speed results in shallow-running baits; a split shot may be added near the barrel swivel to gain more depth; and three, you could consider adding a Ready Release to a line.

A Ready Release is a handy tool enabling a rigged Flat line to be quickly converted to a Down-line. The Release consists of three components: a snap in which you can add a weight, a release mechanism, and another snap through which your line will run. You can achieve a desired depth by simply adding the Release to your line. Use a one or two ounce weight in almost all cases. The versatility of the Ready Release also enables the converted down line to be used in conjunction with a Planer Board. In this example, you can have a down line with a Planer Board in a matter of several minutes with no major modifications to your rigs! As an example: assume a desired depth of 20 feet. Release about fifteen to twenty feet of line; clip the weighted Ready Release to the line; drop the Ready Release twenty feet and then attach the board to the line. Now, let out some line to allow the board to drift to the side of the boat. Behold—A Down-line on a Planer Board!

Variations and opportunities abound when using Flat Lines and Planer Boards. Check out this adaptation: attaching a small float to a Flat line assists in depth control. After identifying the desired depth of your flat line bait, attach the float to achieve your goal. Example: Assuming you want your large Trout to be at a depth of 12 feet, you should attach your float 12 feet above the Trout. You could also add a split shot to achieve your goal. You will still see some fishermen using balloons for this purpose, but they are better replaced by a float.

You may compliment the Planer Boards and Flat lines with Down lines! After setting all the boards and Flat lines, place two or more down lines in your rod holders. One of the tools that will facilitate this is the "T-Bar" from Driftmaster (as previously discussed).

Eventually, you will be able to easily handle eight or more lines. Believe it or not!

Lead Core Trolling

Lead core trolling is one of the most productive means in which to catch stripers from June to September. It involves trolling with a gasoline powered engine. Other equipment requirements are minimal. While the learning curve is short, there are some unique techniques that we will discuss in this chapter.

Successful lead core trolling is a function of depth control. Depth control is comprised of many components including the size, type, and weight of the trolled lure. Of most importance is the quantity of line released from your reel. Let's look at the equipment required to meet the demands of the method.

When examining lead core line, note the various colors. A spool of lead core is 100 yards and consists of ten yard increments each with a different color. Inside the nylon braided line is lead. The strength of lead core varies: 18, 27, 36, or 45 pounds. The strength refers to the nylon not the lead.

If you have used lead core or are considering its use, the first question is, "What is the optimum reel size for lead core?" When selecting a reel, take into consideration which weight line will be used, the length of your leader, and the amount of "backing" line to be placed on the reel. Our choice is the Penn 330 because it's spool capacity is sufficient to hold an adequate amount of mono backing, 100 yards of lead core (a full core), and a thirty ft. fluorocarbon leader. A Penn 320 will work; but, the backing will be limited.

Line counter reel required? No, not necessarily. As we will discuss shortly, the amount of line released will be measured by the number of colors and this will affect the depth of your lure. What about a trolling rod? Here is a suggestion: the Tiger Rod by Ugly Stick; seven ft; medium light; 12 to 30 pounds.

Leader? Yes, a leader is recommended. Tie your lure to a fluorocarbon leader having a strength rating less than your lead core. In other words, if you choose to use 27 pound lead core, your leader strength should be 20 pounds or so. Make your leaders in lengths ranging from 20 to 30 feet.

Knot tying and lead core: anytime you choose to tie a knot using lead core line, you will need to remove two to four inches of lead from the line. This may be done by twisting the line three or four times in the same place. Joining your backing (mono) to the lead core and joining the lead core to your fluorocarbon leader will require a knot or the use of a small swivel. You can join mono to lead core using two clinch knots or two uni-knots. Note: if you choose to use a swivel, use a size that will fit through the line guide.

So, with rod and reel in hand you are off to the Lake for some summer-time trolling. To start your day, you have decided to use a two ounce Mack Farr jig with a six inch trailer. After choosing a location, you begin releasing the jig and line. The safest method for releasing the line is to use patience and release the line slowly; to do otherwise will result in your jig making a rapid descent to the bottom or to a tree. Your trolling speed is 2.50 to 2.75 mph. Your reel has lead core with 27 pounds. You are targeting Stripers suspended at a depth of 35 feet. Under these conditions, you should release seven to eight colors. Here's the rule of thumb: When using a non-buoyant two ounce lure with 27 pound lead core and a trolling speed of 2.5 mph, each color released should result in 3.60 to 4.0 feet per water depth. Working with the same parameters but using a one ounce jig, the rule of thumb is: your lure is sinking at the rate of 3 feet per ten feet of lead core.

Don't forget the "golden rule"—keep your lure above the fish! Stripers look up for food, not down. A useful tool that will help you accomplish this is the depth cursor on your sonar unit. Set the depth cursor at the trolling depth of your lures and, as you troll over the fish, determine whether your trolling depth is adequate.

There are some variables to consider when trolling lead core. The first and significant consideration is wind. Trolling into a head wind will definitely affect your speed and (sometimes your course) and will require more diligence on the part of the Captain. Obviously, a tail wind will have the opposite effect. A rather strong tail wind may prevent you from maintaining the desired trolling speed; the answer to this is to either troll into or perpendicular to the wind. There is one other consideration to ponder and that is your steering. If you find yourself making turns consisting of twenty or greater degrees, there will be more "slack" line on the rod that is on the inside of the turn and this will result in an increase in your trolling depth for that particular lure. You may compensate for this by increasing your speed until you bring the vessel back to a straight line.

Trolling etiquette: Once you find the fish and catch a few—well, you know the rest of the story—you will find yourself "smothered" with other boats—some will be down lining while others will be trolling. Maneuvering through all of these other boats and trying to stay on the course where you have been successful just got a lot tougher. The proper trolling etiquette for arriving boats is to adopt the same trolling direction as laid out by the Captain who originally found the fish.

"What lures should I use?" Maybe a better question is, "what lures should I not use." When trolling with lead core, you will have a plethora of choices including but not limited to: Bucktail jigs with trailers; Bucktail jigs with shad bodies; swim baits; hard plastic lures; saltwater rattle traps; large diving plugs such as Cisco Kids; a jig head with a live Herring; a buck-tail with a Herring. Before you attempt to troll any lure, be sure to determine its weight. Your ability to control the depth of the lure will be the measurement of your success.

Lead core trolling: 1071 to 1041. Every troller should understand the meaning of this phrase. 1071 is the mean elevation of the lake when it is full while 1041 represents the depth of the lake in which "most" trees were topped.

Thus, when trolling outside of creek and river channels, a troller must know the water elevation for the day. Here is an example: assume the lake level is 1065 feet. If most trees were topped at 1041 feet, you can safely assume that the maximum trolling depth for the day is 24 feet—again in non creek and river channels.

When a trolled lure tangles in a tree, should the lure be retrieved? Should you roll-up your lines and return to the tree that's got a grip on your jig? Here is our experience. In those cases where you have been trolling over the trees and your jig is hung, do not attempt to navigate the boat back to the location of the tree. If you attempt to do this, it is very possible some of your lead core line will also be in adjoining trees and you may lose not only the jig but a considerable amount of your lead core. What is the answer? Stay on your original course, tighten the drag, and attempt to muscle the lure out of the tree. Sometimes the jig will come back to you with an attached limb while other times you will lose the jig or the jig and the leader

Most creek and river channels have few trees. This offers a troller an opportunity to safely drop his baits to greater depths and in the hottest water temperatures of the summer this technique can be very productive.

On Lanier it seems most folks troll two lead core rigs. Is it possible to troll more? Yes. Depending on your ability to manage trolled lines, you could troll up to six lines. You can accomplish this through the use of outriggers or you could use heavy/large in-line planer boards.

Before we move on to another subject, it would be prudent to discuss what to do with your catch. Unlike planer board and down line fishing where the fight is limited to about 100 feet or less, a lead core trolled fish will fight over a span of 240 or more feet. By the time it is by your boat, the lactic acid build-up is substantial and its life will undoubtedly be shortened. If you intend to release a trolled fish, consider this. Once you have a fish on, immediately roll up the second line and turn the boat in the direction of the fish. This will shorten the "fighting distance". Once the fish is by the boat take every step to release it in a quick fashion. Also, if you should see a "floater" on the lake, consider picking it up and disposing of it properly.

Umbrella Rigs

Mention U-Rig trolling to some Lanier fishermen and you will get a big scowl while others will offer the double thumbs up. It's a love-hate relationship. Either you love to use them or you swear you will never use them again!

While it may not be exotic, Umbrella Rig trolling is very effective. It is a multi-faceted tool that can be used to locate fish and to catch them as well. Whereas the Rig was once considered a winter/spring tool, it is now used 365 days per year by many fishermen including professional guides.

As with many other methods, the key element of U-Rig trolling is depth control. Trolling speed, trolling patterns, and the weight of the Umbrella Rig directly affect the depth of the rigs. Like other methods, the rigs should be trolled above the fish. Water clarity plays an important role as to your trolling depth. Your equipment will assist in setting the depth of the Rigs.

Equipment: More than likely you will have rods and reels that will work very nicely for Rig trolling. A personal preference for us is to use a line counter reel; however, a Penn 320 or 330 is just as effective. With your Penn 320 or similar reel fully spooled, one pass of the level wind is ten feet. Over time the excessive strain of the rigs will have a negative effect on your reels and you can expect to replace the paw and worm gear frequently.

Ah yes, what to put on the reel? Mono or braid? The popularity of braid is growing exponentially for a number of reasons. First, the diameter of braid is less than mono; so, to reach the strike zone requires less line. Less line allows you to quickly turn and make a second or third pass over a school of fish thus putting you in a position to double or triple up on a school of Stripers that are actively feeding.

Braid, 100 pounds or higher, compares favorably with 50 pound mono with respect to diameter. Heavy duty braid is very helpful when your rig tangles with underwater structure. Using the braid will allow you pull the rig out of the structure with minimal or no damage.

U-rig trolling places considerable stress on both your reel and rod. A popular rod for u-rigging is the medium light or medium heavy Tiger rod. Some Offshore rods work just as well. You will need a rod like these to absorb the frequent surges and sudden changes in the speed and direction of the boat and the force of the strike of a 25 pound Striper seventy feet behind your boat!

U-Rig Retriever: From time-to-time, a U-Rig will latch on to an underwater obstruction. While you may decide to extract the U-rig by pulling it out with your main line, there is another method available. You can purchase a U-Rig Retriever and use it successfully. First, position your boat directly over the U-Rig to hold your main line as vertical as possible. Next, attach the Retriever to your main line and allow it to sink to straight down the hung-up U-Rig. Once the Retriever hooks have engaged the U-Rig, pull it all to the surface.

Umbrella Rigs: With a solid performing rod/reel combination, the next step is the purchase of the rigs. Rigs are made in various weights; some have three arms while others have four. Our recommendation is the four arm, three ounce Umbrella Rig. Furthermore, we suggest that you attach nine lures to each rig. If you have never used Umbrella Rigs, begin by using jigs that weigh three quarters of an ounce. As you master the art of umbrella rig trolling, you will be able to change the weight of the lures.

With the rig in hand, you can attach the lures with monofilament or wire leaders. The length of the leaders is important. Wire leaders are made in different lengths and strengths. If you decide to use wire, go with 20 or 25 pound test and a length of six to nine inches. Mixing the length of the leaders is a good idea as the rig will have more breadth; however, leaders exceeding nine inches will almost always result in more tangles and downtime. Remember that the center leader should be longer than the eight other leaders. The lure on the center of the rig is almost always the one that the fish strike! For that reason, be sure that lure stands out—its hook should be straight; the trailer, if attached, should be properly placed on the hook; it could be a different color; and it could be a different style; it could also have a slightly different weight.

An argument for monofilament leaders: You can and should consider making the leaders with fifty pound monofilament. The mono does not have to be fluorocarbon. This can easily be done with a crimping tool and properly sized crimps.

Make the length of the leader of the center jig line just a bit longer than the other leaders. Note the use of 50 pound mono with crimps. Each leader has a different length. Also notice that six inch trailers have been added to the jigs. This is the most popular and productive umbrella rig on the lake.

Whether you purchase or make the rigs, you should think about presentation. Jigs are popular and can be fitted with or without a blade. Either jig will be effective. While there some guidelines regarding leader lengths, some professional fishermen attach a number of the lures directly to the U-Rig! If you are making your own Rig, shorter leaders (two to six inches) are effective. Again, be sure that your center jig is on a longer leader than the other eight jigs.

What about colors? Initially, it's wise to troll two different looking Rigs to determine which color and trailer scheme is more popular. As an example, on one side of the boat use a white jig with a chartreuse trailer and complement that on the other side with green jigs and white trailers. Yes, you can use shad bodies. Yes, you can use the six inch flappy tails although they are difficult to find. Shad bodies and trailers come in different colors, weights, and length and are readily available. As you can see, your creativity has no limits when making a U-Rig.

Trolling techniques: Now, you are on the water with the rig in hand and ready to begin your successful day on the lake. With the boat moving, place the rig in the water. Each jig should be swimming free of the other jigs. Release the rig slowly to obtain the desired trolling depth.

Maintain a trolling speed of 2.75 to 3.25 M.P.H. and change the speed from time-to-time to learn what the fish are looking for. You can use the same speed schedule whether you are in clear or stained water. Numerous trolling patterns exist; try the "S" pattern and the figure eight patterns. Both of these patterns when used properly will allow the trolling depth of your lures to change. As an example, when turning to port, the rig on that side will drop in the water column while it is moving but its speed is a bit slower. As the Captain turns back to starboard, the rig on the port side will rise and experience a slight increase in speed. This is the "S" method and should be used in wider creeks or open water where the fish are suspended and on the move.

The figure eight method is an extension of the "S" pattern and will allow your rigs to change trolling speed as well as depth. Again, the use of the Umbrella Rig results in a "reaction" strike; therefore, changing speeds and small changes to trolling depths can make a significant difference.

Both the "S" pattern and the figure eight pattern are effective throughout the year.

In the fall and spring Stripers may be found on points and humps. Trolling umbrella rigs over points or on the sides of points is very tedious therefore you should have a good understanding of the depth of your rigs. This holds true for trolling over humps as well. Also, take advantage of your mapping software to orient your trolling pattern to certain contour lines. One of the features of the Navionics software is to highlight shallow water on Lanier with shades of Blue—light blue can be related to water with a depth of less than 30 feet and dark blue can indicate more shallow water.

Throughout this book the importance of depth control has been stressed regardless of your fishing technique. Depth control when trolling Umbrella Rigs is extremely important. Throughout the year Stripers are known to live in small shallow pockets, on lake points and humps, and in open water. Maintaining proper trolling depths and making the proper rig presentation will result in success!

The tool that you need to make important decisions while Umbrella Rig fishing is the Trolling Chart . Please note that the chart assumes: the use of braid, a trolling speed of 2.75 MPH, a three ounce—four arm umbrella rig, and nine three quarter ounce jigs.

FOUR ARM THREE OUNCE UMBRELLA RIG
NINE 3/4 OUNCE JIGS
TROLLING SPEED: 2.7 MPH
TROLLING WITH BRAID

LINE RELEASED	DEPTH IN FEET
50	17
60	18
70	19
80	19.5
90	20.5
100	21
110	22
120	22.5
130	23
140	24
150	25
160	26

Downriggers

Downriggers are just a way to use a heavy lead ball on a stainless steel wire to hold your line at a depth you desire. The balls are typically between 6 and 10 pounds.

There aren't too many boats on Lake Lanier that use Downriggers. That is a shame. Most fishermen use Lead Core line to get their baits to a depth that they prefer. If your boat lends itself to attaching one or two downriggers, you will be pleased with the outcome. They will allow you to get baits or lures into position quickly and eliminate the need for a heavy weight on the line to keep it down when trolling. That makes reeling in your fish much easier and enjoyable. Think about pulling a swim-bait at 25 feet with no weight on your main line.

There are two types of downriggers—manual and electric. They are made by a variety of manufacturers. If you can afford electrics and have a way to hook them up, get them. Most fishermen get tired of turning the crank up and down all day and grow to hate their downrigger. On electrics, when you hook up a fish, you simply flip a switch to bring up your weight and line to get it out of the way. Nothing makes short work of monofilament like sawing it across a stainless steel wire.

Another thing to consider, actually it is essential, is to use rods made for downriggers. They are typically medium weight and have many guides, especially near the tip. The tip of the rod will be more flexible too. This specialized design allows you to properly set the line clip to hold the line in position off of the ball and not exert too much upward pressure on it thus springing the clip prematurely. The clips are pretty much the same as those used on your planer boards, just a bit larger.

When your downriggers are set, you can make sharper turns than you can with lead core and if a fish pulls your line off of the clip, your rod will spring up, a sure sign that something just happened. Use you fish finder to see what depth the balls are at and in Lake Lanier, keep them out of the trees. You can run your baits right through or under bait balls that way and you can be assured that you are at the proper depth. Try running your baits at different depths until you get hit, then move them both to the sweet spot.

As far as selecting weights, make sure they are heavy enough for your trolling speed, watching the angle of the lines as you move. If they are pulling too far back from vertical, either slow down or you need more weight. Shape? Shiny stuff on the weight? Sure, as long as you like it. It probably does not make much difference as your bait is pretty far behind the ball. However, it can't hurt.

If you are so inclined, you can add a clip that attaches to the wire above the ball that has an additional release for another line. This way you can stack additional bait above the one clipped off of the ball, using two or more baits per downrigger. Maybe pull buck-tail off of the ball and a swim-bait off of the upper clip. You can effectively fish four different depths, with precision.

Top-Water

It's the middle of October and you are watching your favorite baseball team participate in the World Series when you cell phone rings. The caller I.D. indicates your fishing buddy is calling. Before you can say "Hello", he is screaming that you have got to get to the Lake—the Stripers are busting the surface everywhere on the south end. I don't know about you but that's an easy decision for me. Give me a Redfin!

When the top water action activity increases on Lanier, it seems that everyone becomes a Striper fisherman. Personal Watercraft, 14 ft flat bottom boats, bass boats, pontoon boats, large cruisers, and center consoles mix it up in what sometimes turns out to be a wild and wooly chase for surfacing fish. However, top water fishing on Lanier consists of more activity than chasing large schools of fish.

There are two types of top water fishing: one, spot and chase and two, targeted fish. Spot and chase, as its name implies, requires the fisherman to run his boat to schools of surfacing fish. Targeting fish with top water lures involves a strategy based on a fishing pattern—the fisherman believes fish are on underwater humps or on long tapering lake points.

Every fall you see folks on the south end of the Lake, engines running in neutral and glassing the water for surfacing fish. Once spotted, the boat rushes to the location and the fishermen usually throw a top water lure. This type of activity usually occurs in October and early November.

Favorite lures include Redfins, Spooks, Chug Bugs, Sammys, etc. This type of activity generally occurs in the morning and late afternoon/evening. The complaint most often heard regarding this method is that at least one boater will approach the school too fast and push the fish down. Our experience with this method is that you can spend a significant amount of time spotting, chasing, and casting and end up with no or few fish.

In October, early November, and May, you can use top water techniques on underwater humps and long tapering points. The most useful tool in this process is your sonar unit, which should be equipped with a mapping function. Use the software to identify the humps and points meeting your criteria. Generally, your targeted areas would be those with 25 feet of water or less. The classic example— the humps that almost always produce are those at the entrance to Young Deer Creek. Your approach to structure/top water fishing is to circle humps while you cast to the center; your approach to points is somewhat similar—cast the lures to the windward side of the point where possible.

Don't spend a lot of time casting to one piece of structure. Limit the number of casts to five to ten. While you are throwing and moving the boat around structure, be sure to look at the sonar. There may be fish stacked up on or near the structure but not willing to sacrifice themselves to you. In this example, you can leave and come back later or you can pull out your Umbrella Rigs and try the trolling method for a reaction bite. Many times these fish need a small "nudge" to turn them on and in those cases the Umbrella Rig is the ticket!

Here is a method that you should consider: when there are two or more fishermen in the boat, position the boat such that the person in the front will throw first to the structure. This person should be throwing a large noise-making lure such as the saltwater version of the Chug Bug; use the blue/chrome to increase your chances for a hook-up. The large lure and its related "chugging" noise will get the attention of any fish in the area and cause them to look up—just in time for them to strike the second lure that passes over them. This second lure should be a Redfin or a Super Spook. The Redfin requires just enough speed to create a "v-wake" while the Super Spook requires the traditional "walk-the-dog" presentation. Should you experience a short strike or a big blow-up on or behind your lure, continue your presentation; do not stop the retrieval process!

The Super Spook "Bleeding Shad" can be a very productive lure. To enhance the lure and to increase your odds of a "hook-up", consider adding a split ring to the nose of the lure and changing the hooks.

Redfins come in different color combinations. On sunny days use blue/chrome; on cloudy days use the "Smokey Joe" color which is two-tone brown.

Whether using a spinning or casting reel, consider using 30 pound braid with a two to three foot fluorocarbon leader. You will be amazed as to the increase in casting distance when using braid.

You can't go wrong with a stiff seven foot rod. Load-up your rod by keeping 12 to 18 inches of line between the rod tip and the lure just prior to casting. The combination of the braid and a stiff casting rod will result in some long casts which many times are necessary. The constant whipping of the lure places significant strain on the knot at the lure—check the knot frequently.

The direction and force of the wind will have a direct effect on top water fishing. Use the wind to your advantage—position the boat whereby you can cast with the wind at your back. Wind will have a direct effect on plankton, small bait fish, large bait fish, and Stripers. Target wind-blown points!

Top-water fishing whether targeting areas or spotting and chasing is not for the faint-hearted. Many times, the big strike occurs when least expected. Use your sonar unit and its software to assist in identifying targeted structure and fish. Also, use a "run and gun" approach to top water fishing.

River Fishing

River fishing is more than just fishing—it's a complete package consisting of steep cliffs, Mountain Laurel, the fall leaf colors, otters, beavers, and deer, and the overriding question of "what is around the next river bend? " Whether spring or fall, the River Experience will beckon your return each year!

The experience of River fishing is completely different than that of your trials and tribulations related to fishing on the South end of the Lake. Less boat traffic and noise contribute to a wonderful setting for trophy Striper fishing.

As you head north of Clarks Bridge searching for a Trophy, there are a few things to consider. First, why are the Stripers "up the River"? Response: they seek a preferred water temperature range, highly oxygenated water, and something to eat.

Fish in the River are comfortable with a water temperature range of 48 F. to 64 F. Water in this temperature range would be expected to have plenty of available oxygen. Their bait of choice is the Gizzard Shad.

The fishing technique identified with Planer Boards and Flat lines is the technique most widely used when fishing in the River. While the technique is similar, you may consider some equipment changes. First, step up your leaders to 20 pounds. If the water is fairly dingy, which many times it is, you may consider tying your hook directly to your main line. If you have the luxury of owning a large number of reels, consider using 25 to 40 pound test for the main line. Because many of us have never boated a trophy Striper, we might not be mentally prepared for the biggest fish of our lifetime. As the Boy Scouts say, "Be Prepared".

In addition to beefing-up your equipment, you will need your Planer boards and a Float or two. Some fishermen use a stinger hook (a treble hook attached to your primary hook). When selecting a hook, match it to the bait you are using. If you decide to use a stinger hook, start with a 3x or 4x.

If you have the time and energy, take your cast net with you. Targeting larger bait fish such as large Gizzards may require a net with a one-inch mesh with additional weight. There will be instances when you will see the Gizzards "flipping" or "tailing". Look for these telltale signs when preparing to throw the cast net.

So, you have your equipment and big baits and you are wondering whether to troll upstream or downstream. Use your electric trolling motor to troll downstream. If you have some trouble keeping the baits deeper in the water column, consider adding split shot to the line. In the fall and winter, maintain ground speed between 0.5 to 1.25 MPH. In the spring, consider increasing the trolling speed.

Before moving on to the next subject matter, here are a few considerations, adaptations, and modifications to River fishing techniques. Give plenty of attention to any "holes" you locate. Stripers will be in these holes facing up-stream patiently waiting for their next meal delivered by the River current. Unfortunately, a surge in the level of wa-ter from several days of heavy rain can fill your favorite hole with silt and create a new hole 100 yards downstream. As you can see, there is the added feature of exploring when seeking the trophy. Give due attention to some of the bends in the River that are bordered by rock cliffs.

Much like saltwater fishing, look for a flotilla of float-ing debris. The floating debris will absorb sunlight and as a result may have a small warming effect on the adjoining water—this small effect may have a big effect on bait and Stripers; so, be sure to move your baits through this area.

If you can identify an area holding a fair number of fish, consider pitching a Shad with a spinning rod to that area or just upstream from that area to enable your bait to naturally swim into the "zone".

Moving further up the River and fishing in more shal-low water and additional current offers another type of fishing technique. Identify the pockets or deeper holes and strategically anchor your boat. Allow the River current to run your boards out to the selected pockets, holes, etc. Po-sition the board above the targeted areas with your bait sitting in the "honey hole". During the day, fish will move in and out of these pockets and holes.

Your success in River fishing will be dependent on your ability to find the Striper holes and the patience to wait for the big strike.

Fishing during the turnover

The turnover can present some trying times on the lake. The fish are actively seeking areas of water that are comfortable for them and eating may not be the first thing that comes to their mind. Some days the fish may be on points and underwater humps while other days they will be chasing bait on the surface. Don't be surprised if you found them suspended at 60 feet in the river channel!

To be successful during the Lake Turnover, you should take top water lures, bait, Planer Boards and Flat Lines, Down-line rods and Umbrella Rigs. Conduct a search pattern early in the morning for top water activity; as time passes use your top water lures on underwater humps, wind-blown points and shallow sand/mud bars. Stick with this pattern through mid-morning then look in 20 to 50 feet for fish that might be catchable with your Umbrella Rigs. You should find some fish either at the mouths of creeks or half-way back in some creeks.

Searching and targeting fish on the south-end of the lake during the turnover can be frustrating; so, why not consider concentrating your efforts to the north-end where fish may be schooling. Look for bait and fish in Little River, Wahoo Creek, Laurel Park, and, of course, the River north of Clarks Bridge. Down-lines, Planer Boards and Flat Lines will be your best bet. Try using some medium Trout and Gizzards in addition to Bluebacks. As we have said before, never leave your Umbrella Rigs at home.

Remember that the oxygen levels are mixed in the water as well as the temperatures, so the fish will be moving around.

VI
Advanced Techniques

Now it's time to add a few tricks to your arsenal. You will be using these techniques in combination with your basic techniques from time to time to generate a bite when the going is tough. The first technique is a Lake Lanier favorite.

Power Reeling

Ah yes, the image of a large, bulky reel—maybe electrically driven, dances across one's mind when considering "power reeling". Fortunately, electrical wires, a fish fighting harness, and a host of bulky fishing equipment does not comprise power reeling on Lake Lanier. As a matter of fact, the phrase refers to a simple fishing technique often used by the professionals.

Power reeling is very effective during the period of June through September. It is so simple that your ten-year old son or daughter can successfully use it after a five minute tutorial.

First, power reeling is an offshoot of Down-Line fishing. Most of the time you will be using a live Herring; although some folks are successful with dead or frozen bait. Using a summer-time method of down-lining a live Herring, send your bait down to a depth below the school of Stripers shown on your sonar unit. Now, begin the retrieval of your terminal tackle. As the bait is pulled through the Stripers, one or more fish will become attracted to this upward movement and will make short order of your Herring.

Let's look at some of the details of this unique fishing method. With respect to equipment, the good news is you should not have to make any purchases. The equipment you use for Down-Line fishing will "fit the bill".

Regarding terminal tackle you should shorten your leaders to about three to four feet. The use of longer leaders will result in an occasional tangled and twisted line. Fourteen to seventeen pound leaders are in order. Twenty pound base line should be used. A two-ounce sinker with swivels will work just fine.

Over the seven to eight year period that Power Reeling has been popular on Lanier, fishing gurus such as our readers offer various views as to the retrieval speed. Our experience is that on any particular day, one school may want the bait retrieved very slowly while another school will bite a quickly retrieved Herring. So, as with other techniques, be flexible and experiment with the reel speed.

As you might guess, the constant up and down movement of your Herring will have two results. First, your live bait can only take so many trips through the band of warm water before expiring and eventually he will become foul hooked. Now, a half dead or completely dead Herring may be used for power reeling; however, a foul hooked bait that forms a spiraling motion while retrieved is not going to catch anything. You can place a small piece of rubber band on the hook to prevent any fouling.

When power reeling, do you set the hook? Good question. Experience shows that you will need to set the hook even when using an Octopus hook. A circle hook is not the best choice for this method, as you are moving the bait too fast.

Be ready to power reel during the summer months. Retrieval speeds may vary. Drop the bait below the school and reel the bait through it. Be ready to set the hook. When setting the hook, take into consideration that there will be some stretch in your mono. Also, replace or re-hook fouled bait.

Jigging

I saw that yawn! Stop it. All of you Herring Heads need to sit up in your chair and pay attention as you learn more about one of the most exciting ways to catch a Lanier Striper.

Jigging has a long and illustrious history. Hundreds of years ago, good folks in the South Pacific and Europe successfully used this technique. Some of the same techniques are in use today right here on Lanier. Heck, it is probably the oldest trick in the book.

Jigging Techniques: Jigging is called different names including spooning, vertical jigging, speed jigging and Japanese jigging. Regardless of the method, the speed, and presentation—depth control and water temperature represent the pivot point for jigging. Water temperature as stated in previous chapters will help you locate fish and identifying their depth will be a major factor when attempting to catch them. Let's look at the characteristics of each technique to determine which might be applicable for Lanier.

Assuming you have located a school of Stripers in the winter, you will be successful jigging a 0.6 ounce or one ounce Flex-It Spoon both of which come in different colors and each has a treble hook in the tail. A Flex-It spoon is designed to flutter and glide when dropped on the Stripers. This method is especially effective during the coldest months as the spoon imitates a dying Threadfin Shad. Once you reach the desired depth, you can choose one or more jigging techniques. Mechanical jigging calls for the spoon to be dropped below the school, the rod is raised with a small arc, and the reel is wound for each cycle. We think you will find the "flutter and glide" drop and the "short and small arc" retrieval methods to be very effective in the winter.

The first thing to remember about summer-time jigging is that it usually involves deeper water—as much as 100 feet; accordingly, one factor to consider is visibility. With respect to the murky waters we would expect at 70 to 100 feet, it would be wise to have jigs with luminous finishes. Color choice is just as important: generally dark overhead conditions call for a dark colored jig while a bright day would call for brightly colored jigs.

In the summer-time, which jigging method is the most successful? Maybe try the following method: drop your jig or spoon to the desired depth, lift your rod about three feet or so, lower the rod about three feet or so *and then* steadily wind-up about two to three turns. Expect to get hit when the jig is in "free fall and fluttering". Yes, often the hit is on the way down. If you think of it, isn't this the way a striper usually sees an easy to catch wounded baitfish. Fluttering slowly to the bottom.

Here's a twist to summer-time jigging. Sometimes, you will be successful by simply reeling the jig or spoon. You may want to consider a twitch or two. Vary your reel speed to determine what works best.

Jigs: What to jig? Answer: at least one hundred or more different spoons and jigs are readily available in different colors, shapes, and sizes. As we mentioned earlier, Flex-it Spoons are effective year-round. Jig Heads with a trailer or a Jig Head with a shad body should be in your tackle box. There are many types of spoons that will work. Today, many spoons and jigs are painted to resemble a specific bait fish. Don't forget Swim Baits—our favorite is the Tsunami Blue Back; although Storm and Calcutta make good products. Cast the Swim Baits and retrieve. Some of the best looking lures include Butterfly Jigs by Shimano.

Not every jig should be attached to your line the same way. In order for some "flutter and glide" jigs to work properly, you may have to attach a split ring or possibly use a loop knot. In other instances, a ball bearing swivel attached to a split ring may be the ticket. Some lures such as Shimano's Butterfly Jigs require assist hooks to be attached to the eye of the lure. Some jig manufacturers suggest that you attach a duo lock to enhance the flutter/glide/dart actions. Of course, a good quality snap swivel reduces line twist.

Equipment: The first rule regarding equipment is: match the gear to your requirement. Heavy gear (rod and reel) can cause premature physical fatigue which in our opinion leads to mental fatigue. Mental fatigue and poor catch results may lead to a disgruntled jigger—this is not the desired result. This must be taken into consideration when choosing both a rod and reel. Hopefully, you already own a rod and reel that may be used for jigging. A 6 ½ to 7 feet rod, medium or medium light, will get you started. Vertical jigging requires some knowledge of the depth of your lure. If you can accomplish this with a spinning reel/rod, you will have an advantage. A bait caster with a line counter will normally put you on the money; and, a fully spooled bait caster without a line counter can also be used with the knowledge that every crossing of the level wind is ten feet.

Line and Leader: Ah, yes—the line. Consider braid. It reduces drag and has very little stretch. Its thin diameter allows for the use of a smaller and lighter reel. Assuming you sign-up for braid, you will need a fluorocarbon leader between 10 and 17 pound test. The size and weight of the lure will help decide which pound test to use.

One day soon, make it a point to rig one of your rod/reels for jigging and leaving it set up that way. Take three to four different lures and test the waters if you have not already done so. You may find a new and exciting way to catch the line sides.

More Trolling Techniques

There is a hot new trolling method that is gaining popularity. This is a fishing technique that is seldom employed for Lake Lanier Striper fishing, but is nonetheless very effective. As you may recall during the summer of 2010, Stripers seemed to have an aversion to live Blue Back Herring. Unlike prior years in which they formed large schools, the Stripers did not school that well. Furthermore, when you were on top of five to twenty five of them, they snubbed their nose at you. This caused most Lanier fishermen to start pulling Lead Core or Umbrella Rigs and some used their Down Riggers more often.

During this period, we employed another trolling technique that can be used in the River, Mid-Lake, or South-Lake year-round that some would try to label as advanced or secret. Why? If you use this method on Lake Lanier, you will likely be seen as a cutting edge fisherman, for at least a while. Then your buddies will be copying you. Again.

The truth of the matter is that you can easily adopt the method discussed below and you will likely catch a few more fish.

This new trolling technique involves the use of only two trolling boards—one port and one starboard. The boards are special ones—dual board planers. By using 100 feet of line from the boat to the board, you can easily troll three lines on each side of the boat. You will be able to troll any assortment of lines including Lead Core, Diving Plugs, and Umbrella Rigs. In the cooler months you can troll live bait with your trolling motor—again, three lines on each side of the boat.

So, you are wondering how this is done. Easy. Either make or purchase a dual-board planer. They are pretty large compared to what you usually see. Attach some form of thin but strong line such as small-diameter braided nylon to the board. Put a different color on the right and left if you are so inclined. Attach the other end of the line to the rail on your T-Top or other strong attachment point fairly high up but reachable; maybe to a radar arch if you have one. If a sturdy high point is not available, rig a steel or aluminum pole and place it in a centrally located rod holder or the hole for a seat. The angles by which the boards are constructed cause them to run parallel to the boat, one to each side.

There are large reels, mostly made of plastic, that have been used on the great lakes for planer and trolling board fishing. They are perfect for this purpose, as they are fixed to the boat and neatly hold the line to the trolling board instead of simply tying it to the boat. Some are a complete unit with a vertical pole mount.

Your big ol' trolling boards are now attached to your boat and next you are going to clip your fishing line to some clips that you let slide down the planer board line to a specific distance.

See, we told you it was easy. Here is what you do. Pay out your main fishing line, be it monofilament, lead core line or a U-rig to the length you want to pull your bait. When finished, attach the line to an orange or black release from Offshore Tackle, which ships the release with a shower curtain ring that opens. So, open the shower curtain ring and place it on the nylon line. Close the ring and allow it to slide almost down to the board. The amount of line you release from the reel establishes the position of your line on the nylon rope. The more line released from your reel, the further down the nylon rope your line will be stationed.

This same process is used for the other one or two lines that you wish to troll on that side of the boat. Normally, the rod with the line closest to the board would be seated in the rod holder closest to the transom. Placing the rods in your holders tipped up at a 45 degree angle or better works too. Believe it or not, Rocket launchers come in real handy when you are using this method.

The benefit of using the trolling boards in the summer and early fall is that you can troll three separate lines on each side of the boat plus two Down Riggers! Normally, you would be limited to two Lead Core lines and two Down Rigger lines. The new method doubles the number of lines! Yeah, I know what you are thinking—this method is the perfect tool for tournaments. The beauty of the system is that two fishermen can handle the entire operation.

You may wish to consider painting your boards orange so that they are visible to other boaters; likewise use a bright colored rope or line for safety purposes. A small bit of reflective tape on the top of the planer board will help you to see it in low light conditions. Also, the tension of the Offshore Release is adjustable by moving the small spring forward/backward.

Before we move on to more discussion on using the boards during the fall/winter/spring fishing seasons, let's look at some distinct advantages. First, there are some significant cost savings by making your own trolling boards versus purchasing six Offshore or Church's boards for approximately $150 to $225. Second, you can easily double the number of trolling lines you would normally use. The orange releases may be purchased for $5.00 each. 100 feet of nylon rope/line is about $4.00. Another consideration—the store bought boards may not be capable of handling your Umbrella Rigs easily.

The beauty of the dual board planers is their versatility. When using live baits and the dual board planers, your lines *will* be significantly farther away from your boat which is a big plus in a small/narrow cove or pocket. You can easily place three live bait lines on each side of the boat; most Lanier fishermen are limited to two planer board lines on each side. Another advantage is that you will no longer have to place a bead on any of your lines. You know that over time, the bead can work against the integrity of the knot connecting the line from the reel to your leader, even if you use a knot protector.

There are more advantages—no longer will you forced to fight your trophy while your board is also on the line. How many fish have you lost because the board hit the fish in the head or dislodged the hook? You will no longer have to chase down your boards after a strike. How many of you have had your boards stolen or lost?

Whew! Not advanced! Very practical! Costs savings! Year-Round use! Catch more fish! Increase your catch ratio! More success! Nuff said!

Keeping a log of your fish

This is one of the activities, pretty much the most important one, which sets apart the professionals from the casual fisherman. A log, notebook, tablet, or somewhere where you record your fishing details is one of the best things that you can do. You will start to see patterns, places, times and preferences over time. These logs should record your catch, the date and time, the environmental conditions such as the time of day, temp, weather, wind etc. You need to know what bait and depth as well.

The human mind is very visually oriented, and if you plot your catches, and busts, over time you will see patterns that work for you. They may not work for someone else, but you know that they work for you. Hey, maybe it can tell what not to do or where not to go. You can mark them on your fish finder, but if you lose that chip or have a data loss…. Well…you know what you will have then.

There is not much more to be said about these logs other than fishermen guard them well. They are worth their weight in gold.

Reeling in your fish

It is pretty much the end of the book and it makes sense in some way to end with bringing a fish to your boat.

I don't think enough time is spent on actually landing your fish. Just think about it this way, you have just spent a lot of time and effort researching, planning, purchasing, installing, travelling, rigging and finally baiting your hook. Fishing takes more time too. Now you have a huge striper on the line. You are reeling it in. Whew! Almost there. Then…Dang! Your hard won fish gets off the hook somehow. It couldn't be you…Could it?

Maybe it was. However, there are a few techniques that you can employ to tip the odds of landing a fish in your favor.

If you watch how a striper strikes after bait you will begin to understand how to keep them on the hook. Your very, very sharp hook.

Initially, a striper will likely strike the bait and then orient it for handy swallowing.

So the first rule is:

Leave the rod alone until the fish is hooked. One of the common errors fisherman make is to jump to the rod and set the hook. This may be important for other species, but odds are you will just pull the bait from the striper's mouth during that period of time when it has struck the bait and when it is actually in its mouth ready to swallow. You will know when a fish is hooked well because your rod tip will bury itself in the water if your drag is set high or it will go screaming off if your drag is set low. You will set the drag according to how you prefer to fish but remember:

Never set your drag high enough to where your line will break. Assuming that you have line that is in top condition and your reels are serviced so that the drags are smooth and not sticky, your drag should be set just under where your line will break or where you will straighten out your hook. Check it frequently and every time you place a rod in a holder when pulling bait. If your drag is too high, your line will break at a spot where it is nicked, at a knot or where it has been abraded somehow.

Some accomplished Striper fishermen leave their drag set very light, allowing the fish to take the bait a bit with little resistance before swallowing it. This works very well too.

Now let's say you fish is hooked and line is screaming off of the reel. Exciting! Before grabbing the rod stop a second to mentally prepare yourself. The fish is hooked; take a few seconds to remember what to do:

Never point the rod tip at the fish. Your rod & reel are designed to keep a fish hooked by allowing you to apply constant pressure on the fish. Think of your rod as a shock absorber. In order to allow the rod to do its job properly, you have to do two things:

Keep your tip up and keep the line tight enough to bend the rod by reeling. This is a huge point to remember. A striper has a very hard mouth. If the fish is hooked in a hard area, it will not be buried into the flesh but riding on just the point of the hook. That is why sharp hooks are important and why you have to keep constant pressure on the rod. So:

Never pump the rod. I know that when we watch fishermen hauling in fish on TV they pull back on their rod, pump the rod toward the fish to gain some line, reel and then pump the rod back. You should not do this for striper.

You will lose fish. Period. Other than a line break or straightening a hook, fish get off your hook by two common methods, both requiring slack line. Slack line is often caused two ways: by you pointing the rod toward the fish and by the fish running toward the boat and you are not reeling fast enough.

When the line is slack, even for a moment, a fish can spit the hook easily if hooked in a hard bony area, as the hook simply falls out. If the hook is into soft flesh, say in the corner of the mouth, during the fight this hole becomes elongated from the pressure. This larger hole is perfect for a hook to slip out of in a slack line condition. Remember the times when you boat a fish and then the hook just falls out? That means you did a great job on a barely hooked fish.

If your line goes slack when bringing in a fish REEL LIKE CRAZY! What just happened is that either your fish broke off, spit the hook, or more than likely is running right at the boat—preparing to spit the hook or figure some other way to break off. You job is to immediately to reel in line to keep the pressure on that hook. Keep that tip up. If the tip bends again, you will know you still have a good hook-up.

Fish cannot swim backward. Remember this if you are using a net. If you position your net properly in front of your fish, it will swim right into it. Never try to net them from behind; you will lose fish because they can swim right out. By the way, if you use a net, get one bigger than you think you will ever need. You will need it.

VII
Some Final Thoughts

We hope that you find good use of the information on these pages and it helps you enjoy your Striper fishing. After all, isn't that what it is all about? This book is small enough to keep on your boat for reference too, so please use it as much as you can.

Also keep in mind that there are more ways and methods to catch striper that are not covered in this book. Fly fishing and cut bait fishing are some of them. Try them too, there are some great experts on the lake that will help you learn. Never stop thinking and improving your skills.

Striper fishing is incredibly addictive because no matter how many fish you catch and no matter how large they are, you will always dream about your next trip to the Lake. It is exciting stuff.

Keep learning about Striper—where they live, when and why they move in certain directions, and why they sometimes will not bite anything you present. To fully understand the Striped Bass, you must understand his world, his needs and requirements, and his movement patterns. We are proud that you have made this book part of that never ending process by letting us help you build some more knowledge and confidence. Our goal was to provide the average Lanier Striper fisherman with some more knowledge and tools that when adopted, will help take that next fishing trip to the next level.

While you are out there, take a friend sometime. More than one Striper fisherman was created by going fishing with one of their friends or with one of the lake guides and hooking their first Lake Lanier Striper. Some of them go out and buy a boat the very next day. It is true, we have the photos.

Be safe and go catch some fish.

ABOUT THE AUTHORS

Capt. Tom Blackburn was born and raised near the Chesapeake Bay where he fished it and its tributaries for Rockfish (Striped Bass) all the while learning and devising many useful and productive fishing techniques and methods. His youthful days on the Chesapeake Bay served as a great platform for plenty of on-the-water-training.

He has fished the Great Lakes for Lake Trout, Smallmouth Bass and Walleye as well as fishing Delaware Bay for Sea trout every chance he could. Every summer Tom and his father launched out of Indian River Inlet and trolled for Albacore Tuna. He refined his trolling methods and skills while fishing out of Chincoteague for both Blue and Yellow Fin Tuna.

Like Tom, Capt. Chuck Kizina has been an avid fisherman since his childhood, starting out by fishing for bluegill in a farm pond with his cousins. He has actively fished waters from the Great Lakes to the Gulf of Mexico as well as fishing waters in the Arctic, Atlantic, Canada and the Pacific Northwest.

Both authors presently reside in Georgia, fishing Lake Lanier primarily for Striped Bass. Based on their similar experiences gained by fishing many of the same waters over the years, they became friends and decided to write this book after observing that many productive fishing techniques that they are familiar with are not commonly known or used on Lake Lanier.

Their book is intended only as a simple guide of some thoughts about basic and advanced fishing techniques and not intended to be all inclusive. They figure that writing a book about these focused tips and techniques will help fishermen of all skill levels catch a few more fish.

For a book that is roughly the price of a fancy lure, they figure it is a pretty good deal.

Notes

Notes

Notes

Notes

9345698R0

Made in the USA
Charleston, SC
04 September 2011